DATE DUE			

Eventing Explained

A Horseman's Handbook

Carol Green
Eventing Explained
Novice Horse Trials

ARCO PUBLISHING COMPANY, INC.
New York

Horseman's Handbooks

TRAINING EXPLAINED
JUMPING EXPLAINED
STABLE MANAGEMENT EXPLAINED
DRESSAGE EXPLAINED
TACK EXPLAINED

Note for American Readers

Some of the terms used in this book will be unfamiliar to
American readers. The Glossary of American Equivalents on
page 96 should be consulted in cases of doubt.

Cover photograph : Gerry Cranham

Published 1978 by Arco Publishing Company, Inc.
219 Park Avenue South, New York, N.Y. 10003

First published in Great Britain in 1977 by Ward Lock Limited,
116 Baker Street, London W1M 2BB, a member of the Pentos Group.

Printed in Great Britain

Library of Congress Cataloging in Publication Data

Green, Carol
  Eventing explained.
    1. Eventing (Horsemanship)   I. Title.
SF295.7.G73   798'.24   77-24609
ISBN 0-668-04383-0
ISBN 0-668-04390-3 pbk.

Contents

Introduction

Eventing is a sport that over the past few years has become more and more popular. It is the best all-round test of the horse's training, as he must be calm and obedient enough to perform a dressage test, while at the same time showing courage and the ability to jump both across country and over show-jumps. It is also a test of the rider's courage, fitness and technique.

It is my intention in this book to assist the rider and novice trainer who wishes to take up this sport, beginning with the very basic competitions and finishing with the horse's first horse trial. A good introduction for both rider and horse may be gained by competing in Riding Club one-day events or, if the competitor is under eighteen, in Pony Club events. In America the age limit is twenty. Several of the more prominent international three-day event riders began their careers in the Pony Club. Pony Club and Riding Club events are of a similar standard.

The British Horse Society's Novice Trials and U.S. Horse Trials consist of three main tests: dressage, show-jumping and cross-country. Dressage is a preliminary test lasting about six minutes, designed to display the standard of a horse's basic training on the flat. The show-jumping test is taken over a course of eight or ten fences (ten to twelve in the U.S.). The courses are normally well built and include one or two combination fences; in the British novice class no fence will exceed 3ft 9in (1.14m). Cross-country tests are taken over a course of one and a half to two miles and comprise up to eighteen well-built, solid fences. This will require a bold horse with confidence in his rider and the ability to jump solid obstacles at speed; the height of the fences in the novice class will not exceed 3ft 6in (1.07m).

If you wish to compete in B.H.S. events you must first register your horse, and yourself as owner, with the British Horse Society (at the National Equestrian Centre, Stoneleigh, Kenilworth, Warwickshire CV8 2LR). To be eligible a horse must be 15 hands high or over and five or more years old. This is a precaution against the competing of untrained riders, attempting to force equally untrained horses to perform under conditions which are far too strenuous.

To be eligible, the rider must be sixteen years old or over; an aspirant to show-jumping and cross-country competitions who has begun eventing in the Pony Club will be able to progress to adult horse trials as he or she becomes too old for Pony Club activities.

In the United States the official eventing organization is the U.S.C.T.A. (United States Combined Training Association at 1 Winthrop Square, Boston, Mass. 02110). You have to be a member in order to compete in sanctioned competitions of Open Training Division level and above. Their rule book states the various requirements and both the horse's and the rider's ages in different divisions. The rider must be fourteen or older for the Preliminary Division and twelve or over for the Open Training Division. As to the horse, there is no height requirement in these competitions, but for the Preliminary Division and above the horse must be five years or older.

The Preliminary Division is the approximate equivalent of the B.H.S.'s Novice Trials; the cross-country course covers a distance of between one and a half to two miles (2,800–3,600m) over twelve to eighteen fences, and the fences are similar in height to the British ones. The Open Training course has between twelve and fifteen fences over a distance of one to two miles (2,000–3,000m).

1 Choosing the horse – and rider

Choice of horse for eventing

Good competition horses come in many different shapes and sizes. The crucial characteristics of successful horses, however, are courage, an instinct for self-preservation, and a natural ability for jumping. The event horse also needs a calm temperament and the naturally good paces necessary to produce a good dressage test.

I prefer to begin the training of the horse for eventing as a four- or five-year-old; the type of horse that I look for and would consider buying is one that would perform and be well placed in a working-hunter class. In this way I am assured at least that the horse will have good conformation, quality, manners and good action. Above all the horse must be sound. With a potential event horse, stress to your veterinary surgeon that you wish to use the horse for horse trials. He may well recommend that the horse should have a blood test and an X-ray, and it is well worth the added expense at this stage to avoid the possibility of being disappointed if the horse should prove to be unsound for the work required of him once training has begun. Even at Riding Club and Pony Club level, eventing is very taxing for both horse and rider. It is a gruelling test of all-round fitness and stamina.

As a novice trainer competitor it is unlikely that you will have the wisdom or experience to make your own choice of horse, and it really is worth taking expert advice in your selection. If you are fortunate in having tuition from an experienced trainer, I strongly recommend that you consult him and ask if he would be willing to help you find a suitable horse. Bear in mind that you need to find not only the right type of horse, but also a horse well suited to your own level of ability and experience.

The event rider

The event rider needs to be a good all-round equestrian, with enthusiasm, patience and an easily asserted sense of humour, together with courage and determination. Impatience and ill-temper will quickly convey itself to the horse, and will result in confusion on the part of the horse and failure on that of the rider.

If a good dressage test is to be achieved, the rider must learn to develop a correct seat and thus ride by balance and feel, using only the most subtle aids. I have discussed the requirements of the rider more fully in another book in this series, *Dressage Explained*, and they are the same for this phase of the competition as they are for the full-time dressage competitor. The event rider must be flexible enough also to acquire expertise in show-jumping and cross-country riding. Indeed, I think it is helpful if the rider has had some previous competitive experience in show-jumping before he takes up eventing; surprisingly enough, the weakest aspect of many event riders' performance is in the show-jumping phase.

The rider must be bold as well as skilled. My own feeling is that boldness and courage can be developed as the rider improves his skill and technique, as fear is most often fear of the unknown. I would therefore suggest to all hopeful event riders that they should spend time learning the basic skills. Develop an independent seat; ride as many different horses as possible; go hunting; compete in hunter trials, and then begin on real eventing, first with the small local events, gradually working up to the bigger, more demanding official trials. You should gain in ability and confidence with each new stage reached and mastered, until your courage becomes so much a part of you that it stays with you, no matter how daunting a course you have to tackle.

2 Early lessons

The aids and their importance

The aids are the means of communication between the horse and the rider. They are the most important link between rider and horse, and so essential to successful training that we must consider them first of all. The aids comprise the rider's body, seat, legs, hands and voice, known as the 'natural' aids; artificial aids are martingales, whip and spurs.

It is important that the horse learns to respond instantly to the rider's aids, first during training on the flat, and later over fences. The horse should ultimately develop sufficient confidence in his rider to obey all instructions at once, and go where the rider intends him to go. Throughout training, the rider demonstrates what he requires of the horse by the association of ideas. A simple example is seen in the stable, when a trainer presses his hand to the horse's side with the word 'over'. The horse gradually associates the word with the touch of his trainer's hand and will learn to move over. When a horse shows that he understands a newly taught instruction he should be rewarded with a pat and a kindly spoken word.

The means of communication between rider and horse are by touch — that is, with the horse's reaction to the rider's seat, legs and hands. The driving or 'pushing' aid is applied by the rider's body and seat through the bracing of his back muscles, by the legs through closing the inside of the lower leg against the horse's sides, and the hands by guiding the horse and regulating the energy created by the seat and legs. The voice, spurs and whip may be needed at times and are used as supplementary aids. The rider must develop a 'feel' for the horse's movement, and be able to anticipate any evasion on the horse's part, which he will counteract by use of his legs in conjuction with the reins. With practice and determination the rider can develop such coordination that he can use legs and hands independently of each other. When jumping, loss of balance on the part of the rider may cause the horse to incur penalties either by refusing or by knocking down a fence. To handle the reins well − a minimum of interference with maximum control − and to achieve the best performance of which the horse is capable, is possible only if the rider is dedicated and strives to improve the depth and independence of his seat, and acquires real suppleness and balance.

'Good hands' − hands which are sympathetic yet effective in giving signals to the horse for precision and control — can be acquired only by a rider who is capable of maintaining the depth of his seat, causing no loss of balance and rhythm on the part of the horse, and gradually building up harmony between man and mount.

The simple aids are used diagonally. For example, to turn to the right the rider should look to the right, place the right leg at the girth and the left leg behind the girth, and feel with the right rein so that the horse is also looking to the right. The left rein is then relaxed to allow the horse to go to the right, but contact is not lost and the horse maintains perfect balance. When making any turn or change of direction it is important for the rider to look in the desired direction so that his weight instinctively follows the movement of the horse. This will make it easier for the horse to respond to the aid.

A transition is a change of pace or direction − for example from walk to trot, trot to canter, and canter back to trot. A transition should be carried out smoothly, with the horse maintaining regularity of stride up to and following the transition. The secret of good transition is to prepare the horse well in advance so that he is really concentrating on you and ready to be obedient to your aids. The rider must sit still and upright in the saddle, close both legs inwards, resist a little with the hands, but as he feels the horse 'give' lighten the hand and ride him forwards. The rider may find that in a downward transition − that is, from trot to walk, or canter to trot − the horse sometimes loses impulsion. This may be because the rider, having used the aids for the transition, was not sufficiently quick to recover and lighten the hand, and to use his legs to send the horse energetically forward. Transitions are important, both at the slow and at the faster paces, and it is well worth while practising until the horse and rider are able to carry them out precisely, smoothly and without fuss.

Some people are naturally very well coordinated and will have little difficulty in the correct application of the aids. Others may find them more difficult. If you are one of these, I strongly recommend that you go to a qualified instructor and take a course of lessons on the lunge. It is better if you can arrange not to ride your own horse as you will find it easier to concentrate on improving your own seat, balance, suppleness and coordination, without worrying about the horse's performance. If you combine the lessons with a course of gymnastic suppling exercises, you should find that your use of the aids and your seat are greatly improved when you return to your own horse.

Putting the horse to the aids

In the early lessons we are looking for good free forward movement with the horse working calmly, obediently and actively. It is important therefore that he understands the aids and responds to the leg effortlessly at the slightest indication from the rider. By systematic and regular work it is possible to develop the horse's natural paces so that he will perform when asked, showing the lightness and presence with which nature has endowed him. It is important for any young horse to enjoy all his work. Never school him for so long that he becomes tired and bored with exercises. Hacking is good all-round exercise, giving the horse zest while providing some relaxation from the more formal schooling, and at the same time helping to develop his balance with a rider, especially if work up and down hills can be included, which will promote muscular development as well.

I like my novice horse to hack out three or four days a week for up to one hour at the most, while being schooled two or three times a week. Formal lessons at home should last for up to half an hour each, but not more; in this way the horse will suffer no excess strain at this early stage in his training and will not become bored by too much routine work.

In order that you may increase the suppleness, athletic ability and obedience of your horse it is necessary for you to be aware of the various school movements, loops and serpentines which are ridden at all paces – and to practise them.

These school movements are normally ridden on a single track, changing the rein by turning down the centre and going to the opposite track, riding loops and circles, performing turns on the forehand, changes of rein within the circle, voltes, serpentines, large and small loops, the *demi-pirouette*, and the simple change of leg. All these movements should first be practised at the slow paces; take your time, and prepare well so that your horse really understands what you expect him to do. With this precision work you may find it helpful to carry a schooling whip to reinforce your leg aids and increase your horse's response to and understanding of your aids. As the horse's balance improves, you may progress through to the trot, putting the movements together in various sequences to add variety to the task. Very often the horse tends to lose impulsion on the turns, and this must be anticipated: ride him energetically and firmly forward so as not to lose the rhythm of the stride, thus maintaining the impulsion coming from behind and forestalling any shortening of stride on the turn.

I have found it helpful to the horse in all stages of his training to lunge him two or three times a week before beginning the ridden work. On the lunge the horse is able to develop his own balance without having to adjust to the rider's weight; working on a true circle he is in a good position to develop a rounded top line, using his back muscles without being hampered by the rider. It is also useful for you to be able to study him from the ground. The trainer must lunge the horse on as large a circle as is possible to avoid any unnecessary strain on the hind legs or back – a good size would be approximately 60ft (20m). Lungeing is particularly helpful if the horse is a little fresh, as it allows him free expression without harming himself or his rider. I usually let my young horses work fairly actively on the lunge at the beginning of a session, and I do not mind if they have a buck or a bit of a canter; I feel that this freedom is important for their morale if obedience is going to be insisted upon when they are ridden. After allowing two or three lively minutes on the lunge, I then start to insist that the horse settles, and develops a regular and calm pace without losing rhythm and impulsion.

The basic paces of the horse are important, and this first stage in training should not be skimped or hurried. Only if the groundwork is thorough will the later stages of training develop successfully. His mouth should be closed with a relaxed jaw (if the horse resists in his mouth and sets his jaw, the bit will be held crookedly and it will be impossible for the rider to achieve the best possible performance). The trot should be regular and rhythmical, with the horse lengthening and shortening his stride when asked. Sometimes one finds horses that seem to 'chew' the bit, making their mouths very wet. This is not correct, contrary to what many people think. The bit should be held lightly in the mouth, the weight of both reins being absolutely even. If the rider imagines one ounce of weight in each rein the contact will be good. The rider should not have two pounds in the left hand and nothing in the right.

Once the horse is moving freely forward, calmly and obediently in this early work, I suggest that the trainer should introduce some initial work with ground rails.

Lungeing

Lungeing is beneficial to the horse in that it helps to develop suppleness, balance, muscles, coordination and obedience. Since horses learn by habit all training must be systematic. If an assistant walks the horse in a circle around the trainer, leading the horse from the outside of the circle so that the link between the horse and trainer is not interrupted, the horse will quickly learn the first principle of work on the lunge. The horse must then learn to respond to the trainer's command to 'Walk on', walking on a circle with the trainer encouraging him forwards. Continue on the circle, taking care not to get in front of the horse. All work must be done by the trainer equally on both reins; for your first few sessions with an inexperienced and probably not very fit horse, five minutes on each rein will be ample.

Here are some points which you should remember when lungeing your novice horse:

1 Always work on as large a circle as possible approximately 60ft (20m) in diameter, so that you put the minimum strain on the horse's hind legs. Small circles will cause discomfort and strain — and disobedience.

2 Ten minutes' lungeing each session is sufficient at first, gradually increasing to about thirty-minute sessions. Many horses' natural paces are shortened and impaired through lungeing for too long and on too small a circle.

3 To cultivate a pleasant working association between trainer and horse, the trainer should reward the horse at the end of each lesson by halting the horse, going out to him on the circle and giving him a pat on the neck while telling him he has done well. Never allow the horse to come in to you as he may do it when you do not want him to.

4 When the horse is able to work well in the walk and trot on the lunge, changes of tempo may be introduced to help make his back more supple. Changes of tempo are the change of pace within the paces: for example, when the horse is in working trot, he is asked to lengthen his trot for a few strides, then to shorten it, and finally to return to the working trot. This can be done repeatedly for a few minutes and should assist the horse in his basic training and help him to develop a greater degree of balance.

5 I do not think it is helpful to work the horse in canter on the lunge, except perhaps with a very experienced trainer. It is much more difficult to maintain control in the canter, the horse is likely to become unbalanced and injure himself, and possibly strain his hocks or tendons. If, on the other hand, your horse comes out a little fresh one morning and offers to canter on the lunge, do not pull him up immediately, but allow him to go forwards and then quietly ask him to return to trot.

6 Not all trainers would agree with me, but I think that for all of the lunge work so far, best results will be achieved if side reins are

A young rider has brought her novice horse to a square and attentive halt by careful use of the aids.

Good even work over ground rails. The horse is moving freely and regularly over three rails, an exercise that will achieve balance and rhythm.

It is essential to school the horse at home in a dressage arena so that both horse and rider can become accustomed to working in a confined area. A ground rail placed in front of a small upright fence assists the horse in finding a correct take-off stride.

fitted. They are simply support reins, which should run from the bit to the roller, and they should be of equal length. The side reins replace the rider's hand, give the horse something to seek and go towards, and encourage a good head carriage. It is important, however, that they are not adjusted too short.

7 Work over trotting poles can be very helpful. Arrange the poles on the circle, placing them between 4–5ft (1–1.5m) apart, so that the horse meets them as part of his lunge area. The poles should encourage the horse to lower his head and neck, relax his back and move with a round outline. Notice the action of the inside hind leg: if the poles are well placed and the horse is working in a calm rhythm, the inside hind leg should step into the centre space between each pole.

8 When the horse works confidently on the lunge, some simple jump work may be introduced. Jumping on the lunge gives the trainer the opportunity of studying the outline that the horse makes

When teaching a horse to jump, it is a good idea to give it some lunge work without the rider in the saddle to develop its balance unhampered.

in flight, to discover whether he is flat in his back or has a tendency to rush, or, with luck, that he has been blessed by nature with a round outline. Jumping on the lunge allows the horse to develop balance naturally without being restricted or hampered by the rider in any way. (When working the horse over fences on the lunge the side reins should be removed so that the horse has complete freedom of his head and neck). Place your fence on the outside edge of the circle with a sloping rail on each side of the fence to prevent the lunge line getting caught. Make sure that in flight over the fence you allow your hand to move forward in the direction of the movement so that you do not hamper the horse. It is better to work the horse over low spreads, thus encouraging him to jump with a round back, than to force him over high upright fences.

Work over ground rails

The rails should be placed on the ground approximately 4ft 6in (1.4m) apart for a horse about 15.2 to 16 hands. Ground rails help the horse to look down to the ground while maintaining a regular rhythm in his stride, and encourage him to use the muscles in his back correctly. With these exercises, always be aware of the horse's condition and remember that he must be reasonably fit before undertaking new work to help develop his muscles.

Begin working with just one pole, and when the horse is moving calmly over it increase the number of poles to three. Start at a regularly paced walk, letting the horse adjust his balance while the rider maintains the lightest possible rein contact. The horse should not be 'held up' by the rider's hands. When the horse has gained confidence just walking over the rails, he can be asked to trot over them, still with the lightest possible rein contact. At this stage the pole must be actually on the ground — raised poles, or cavalletti, can be dangerous. When the novice horse is made to trot over even slightly raised poles, his muscles are being put under too much strain. In these early lessons it is essential to keep a definite aim in mind so that at each stage you feel that you have kept the confidence of your trainee — a confidence which has been gained by degrees.

Turn on the forehand

I have already mentioned the turn on the forehand; the time has come for a more detailed explanation of the movement. It is one of the first movements that the young horse must master before he will be able to give the best response to the rider's leg aids. Turn on the forehand, in which the horse pivots on his forehand while his hindquarters describe a half circle, not only teaches him to respond more positively to a rider's aids, but also gives the rider control of the hindquarters. This is essential when out riding in country districts as without doubt you will need to open and close gates on farm land.

The exercise is begun at the halt. In a turn on the forehand to the left, the rider uses the left rein and left leg which should vibrate and ask the quarters to move away from the left vibrating leg. The rider's right leg and right rein are a balance or support aid; the right leg prevents the horse from stepping backwards, and the right rein keeps the horse from wandering forwards. The horse should neither step backwards nor forwards, but it is considered a lesser fault if he steps forwards. The novice horse must be ridden firmly forward after completing the turn, so that he does not lose his forward impulsion or begin to anticipate the movement. When first teaching the horse this exercise I do not usually try for a complete half-turn, but for a quarter-turn, only asking the horse to make two or three steps before allowing him to walk forward. In this way the horse will learn the movement without fear or confusion, and is less likely to evade you or stiffen his back.

Shoulder-in

This is a movement in which the horse moves forward and sideways, bent round the rider's inside leg (in shoulder-in right, the rider's right leg), the horse's body bent away from the direction in which he is moving. The horse must maintain the rhythm of the pace — walk or trot — moving forwards and sideways with regular steps. It is a movement not to be attempted without an experienced person to help you. The aids are: the inside leg at the girth, which

Right shoulder-in, followed by a half-pass to the right. These schooling exercises will help to make a horse supple.

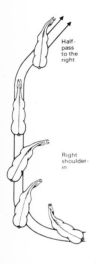

Half-pass to the right

Right shoulder-in

indicates to the horse to move forwards and sideways maintaining energy; the outside leg behind the girth, which controls the hindquarters. The inside rein indicates the bend to the inside while the outside rein controls the speed of the movement. It is best to begin the movement by riding a circle and riding shoulder-in from a tangent of the circle. With a young horse always ride a circle or go away on a diagonal line when the shoulder-in steps are completed.

The shoulder-in is a suppling exercise for the horse and encourages him to bend and flex the three main joints of the inside hind leg, that is, the stifle, hip and hock. The movement also has a good effect on the horse's back and helps to free the shoulders. In the preliminary dressage tests undertaken by novice event horses, such movements as shoulder-in are not included. I believe, however, that it is such a useful and beneficial schooling exercise for the horse that it is nevertheless worth including the movement in schooling sessions.

A more detailed explanation of these schooling exercises and dressage movements may be found in *Dressage Explained*. Once your event horse has competed successfully at novice level and is ready to advance, upgrading to intermediate and advanced competitions, it will be essential for both trainer and horse to improve their understanding and work at a more advanced level of dressage. It is not my intention in this book, however, to take the young horse beyond the stage of novice B.H.S. or US horse trials.

The dressage arena

The dressage arena for novice trials is 66ft (20m) by 128ft (40m). It is important to accustom your horse to being schooled in an arena of this size. You must be very clear on all school figures and movements so that you are able to ride the test well without worrying about where the letters are or what the correct shape of the movement should be.

In any dressage competition, including one-day events, the test is ridden from memory. It is important to learn your test well in advance. Practise on your feet first, and then ride some of the movements on your horse. It is better to practise the complete test on a friend's horse that is not competing, in order to avoid the risk of your own horse beginning to anticipate your aids and perhaps producing a movement a little too early.

Accuracy is important, and it is well worth your while learning to ride school figures with precision, so that you may gain maximum marks for this phase of the event. In America some elementary trials allow for a 'caller', but it still makes for a better ride if the test is memorized instead. A good straight entry is also important. Ride round the outside of the arena, and make your turn into it at A marker deep enough so that you can ride straight down the centre line. Sometimes in a competition the X marker is marked by a little mound of sawdust, and sometimes by white paint on the grass. I have often seen novice horses go down the centre line and stop short of X because they have seen the white mark and are nervous of stepping on it. This, therefore, is something else to practise at home – making a straight entry and halting *on* X with sawdust or paint. At many horse trials the centre line is simply a mown strip of grass, in which case it should not cause you any difficulty, but I would advise nevertheless that you practise your entry, establishing a square halt and a good salute.

The dressage markers are arranged around the arena as follows: A, K, E, H, C, M, B, F. I find a helpful way to remember them is to say the following little ditty, '*A*ll *K*ing *E*dward's *H*orses *C*all *M*e *B*lessed *F*ool'. On the centre line you will find the letters D, X and G. Given below is a diagram of the novice arena.

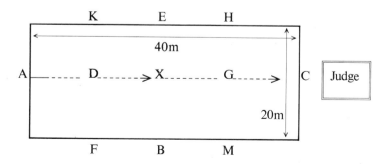

3 Teaching the horse to jump

In these early lessons your aim is to win the confidence of your horse. Encourage the horse to enjoy jumping and to develop confidence in his own ability, while establishing a good style. The novice horse must not be overfaced, that is to say, he should not be urged to jump obstacles that are too big for him so early in his career.

For all jumping work it is advisable to fit brushing boots all round and also to use over-reach boots in front. This is just protective clothing for the horse should he by any chance fall unbalanced and strike into himself.

Place ground rails and small fences in such a way that they will encourage him to jump them with ease. Try to arrange as many variations as possible, using a placing rail to assist the horse in finding his way to any obstacle effortlessly and confidently, knowing where he should come to in his take-off stride. A simple arrangement is to put a 1ft 8in (50cm) high placing rail about 18ft (5.5m) before a small obstacle approximately 2ft 6in (75cm) high.

The horse and rider approach at a trot, trot over the first element, continue at a canter and jump the second obstacle (see diagram below). Numerous trot and canter exercises can be built around this arrangement.*

For jumping you should shorten your stirrups 3–4in (7.5–10cm) from the length you use when riding dressage. Doing so enables your weight to be absorbed at the knee and into the

<   5·50 m   >

* For greater detail, see *Jumping Explained.*

stirrup irons, so that the angles in front of the hip, behind the knee and in front of the ankle are slightly more closed than they are in a normal riding position on the flat. You will improve your seat, as well as the horse's performance, by work over small grids and combination fences, developing an increasingly independent seat, which allows the horse to jump with ease, less hampered by your weight.

Loose-schooling over fences

This is another very good way to teach the horse to jump with confidence. Loose-jumping helps to develop the necessary muscles and encourages the horse to use the full freedom of his head, while at the same time allowing for the rounding of his back and the required folding of his legs for the jump.

A good arrangement for loose-school jumping is to have two fences, an upright followed by parallel bars, 21ft (6.5m) away, both fences to be approximately 2ft 6in (75cm) high (see below).

Combination fences keep the horse mentally alert. Following the upright jump with a spread will encourage the horse to use his shoulders and will lighten his forehand at the first element. The comfortable distance of 21ft (6.5m) to the spread will allow the horse to stretch out and jump in good style over the second element.

Developing courage and initiative: hunting

One of the best ways of developing the courage and initiative of the novice event horse is to ride him in the hunting field. Before he is introduced to hunting, however, he should be thoroughly established in the initial training I have already described, and completely obedient to the rider's aids. There is a risk of spoiling his mouth if obedience and confidence in the rider have not become habit with the horse. In Britain the hunting season lasts from November through to April; the eventing season begins in March with the spring trials and recommences in August for the autumn events. As the seasons of these two sports tend to overlap, I prefer to have one or two seasons' hunting behind the horse before I begin a serious training programme for the eventing season. If, on the other hand, you intend to produce your horse in Pony Club or Riding Club events first, before beginning on the official horse trial events, then a light season's hunting will be perfectly all right as these events normally take place in the summer. Indeed, I normally prefer to hunt a four-year-old lightly, give him a rest in the spring and continue his training through the summer, doing just a few local competitions for experience. The following winter I hunt him again and produce the horse in his first Riding Club events the following June; if all goes well the horse should be ready to begin novice horse trials in the autumn. In the US the eventing season varies from region to region according to the climatic conditions.

Some of my readers may not have had the opportunity to hunt before, so I will explain a little more clearly exactly what is involved and why it can be beneficial to the novice horse. If you intend to hunt for the first time, seek advice from someone experienced as it can be an expensive undertaking; certain rules and conventions need to be followed as far as manners, dress and behaviour are concerned. If possible, arrange to accompany somebody experienced on your first few outings so you are able to follow his example without worry or embarrassment; you will soon learn the do's and don'ts of the hunting field.

The fact that the horse is well established in his basic training and responds well to your aids makes it easier for you to observe commonsense precautions at the first meet. Keep the horse well under control, and stay at the edge of the crowd. At the actual meet keep your horse facing the hounds. An inexperienced horse will feel excited by the atmosphere of other horses and people and

The horse's balance (and that of his rider) will be much improved by
work over hilly ground: this steep slope should be ridden with care.

Continual calm schooling over unfamiliar and awkward obstacles will teach the horse not to be surprised by anything new.

Training for the cross-country phase of a one-day event. The author negotiates an open ditch followed by a post-and-rail fence. Fording a stream at a Pony Club hunter trial. Always remember to introduce your horse to water with great care and control.

After hunting, cross-country fences like this one should present no problems. Here Carol Green jumps a hedge on her horse Miss Cheetah.

may strike out at the hounds which run behind him while he is standing still. Ride round the edges of all fields planted with crops and do not gallop or jump unnecessarily. On the first few occasions do not stay out for more than two hours. Dismount half a mile from your box or trailer (or from home if you have ridden to the meet), slacken off the girth and walk your horse back to the box or trailer. The horse will be tired after such exertion and should be rested the next day, but he should be led out for twenty minutes to work off any stiffness.

In the hunting field the horse will encounter unfamiliar obstacles, so it is best to accustom him to such jumps beforehand; it is also useful to practise in the company of an experienced horse. Sometimes water presents a particular problem. Before taking a young horse over it for the first time do make certain that the bed of that particular stream or wide ditch is sound. In all the novice horse's training for cross-country work it is advisable to have an older and more experienced horse to set an example when it comes to jumping obstacles that are unusual, and as far as hunting is concerned it also teaches him not to get over-excited when jumping in company.

Further schooling: jumping

Although experience in the hunting field will help the novice horse to develop his courage and initiative, it is important to remember that he still is a novice and has much to learn. Hunting does tend to make the horse jump a little flat, and it sometimes gives him false courage; when asked to jump alone in cold blood he may not have the same courage as he had in the hunting field. The best way to develop the horse's judgement of stride and his agility between and over jumps after a season's hunting, is to work him over small combination fences, while at the same time continuing his dressage training. I like to start each day with a little work on the flat so that the horse settles, becoming obedient and responsive to my aids, and then on three days a week to follow this with work over small fences. Work progressively by using low and varied combination jumps. In the early lessons it is better to increase the spread of a fence rather than its height. The horse will learn to jump a fence smoothly and the exercise develops confidence in both rider and horse. The rider will benefit by strengthening his seat and feeling more secure in the saddle. When setting up combination fences for training purposes it should be remembered that an upright fence will encourage a horse to lift his shoulders, while spread fences encourage him to stretch out and to round his back. Careful planning of fences for use at trot and canter will assist the horse to jump with increasing skill and to progress to more demanding fences without loss of style.

The first exercise illustrated here will help the horse to use his shoulders correctly, with rounded back and balanced stride. Lay a pole on the ground 22ft (6.7m) from a small upright fence 2ft 6in (76cm) high. Place another pole 22ft (6.7m) from the upright. Beyond the second ground rail erect a small spread fence 2ft 6in (76cm) high by 3ft (90cm) wide and 23ft (7m) from the last ground rail. The first ground rail, used for the non-jumping stride, will help the horse to correct his canter stride; the little upright at the short distance of 23ft (7m) will help to lighten his forehand and encourage him to jump with accuracy using thrust from his hindquarters.

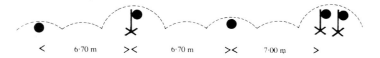

The second ground rail will again check the canter and ensure that the horse meets the spread jump well.

Hunting may make a young horse a little impetuous, and the next exercise will help to steady him, so he will meet his fences properly balanced and without signs of rushing. Place the rails on a circle, a trotting stride apart. If you can lay them down a little way away from other fences etc., you will be able to go straight from jumps to poles, varying the horse's training programme by working around the fences and then going over to the poles on the ground to check the regularity of the pace at the trot, without having to stop and prepare the next exercise in between.

Another exercise I have found useful is to place the ground rails on a circle 4ft 6in (1.4m) apart, with a trot fence at the end of the rails. It is particularly helpful to a young horse, who easily becomes unbalanced. The ground rails set on a circle will encourage extra thrust from the inside hind leg. The horse which has a tendency to run in trot will develop a more positive and well-paced trotting stride. The action of coming out of a corner or out of a circle to progress then on a straight line, still using ground rails, and to finish with a spread fence about 18ft (5.5m) from the last rail will train a horse to jump in good style, to land in a balanced manner and thereby to improve his recovery strides after the fence.

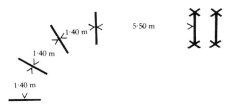

As much variety as possible should be made in these schooling lessons. When the horse is able to jump small combination fences from trot and canter, it is a good idea to set up a small course of show-jumps to practise over. Try to build an inviting course with the fences as solid in appearance as you can make them. There are four main types of obstacle: upright, parallel, staircase and pyramid fences. If possible, incorporate at least one of each into your course, making sure that the first two fences are simple and inviting. When jumping the novice horse over his first series of fences you should take your time and take from the trot those jumps which you think he will jump better from the trot. Make wide turns so that the horse can maintain his balance without strain. It is very important at this stage of his career for the horse to enjoy jumping, so never ask too much of him, or go on too long with your training sessions. A bored horse is a careless horse, and one that will not give of its best.

A small jumping course at home. The horse can make tighter turns once confidence over a variety of fences has been gained.

Combination fences and comfortable distances

In all jumping competitions, whether across country or in show-jumping, it is inevitable that you will meet combination fences. These are a test of the horse's suppleness, balance and athletic ability. If your work at home has been on sound lines they should not cause you any undue worry. As a competitor and trainer it is vital, however, that you are able to gauge distances, so that when you meet with a problem competitively you will know how to deal with it. You should school your horse at home over every possible distance, using simple, low, gymnastic-type fences, so that he grows in confidence and develops the balance and athletic ability necessary to tackle combination obstacles. The distances given below are measured from the face of the landing side to the face of the take-off side of each fence in a combination.

Two vertical jumps set at 26ft (8m) apart allow one longish non-jumping stride.

Two vertical jumps set at 36ft (11m) apart allow two non-jumping strides.

Two parallels placed at 24ft (7.3m) apart allow one non-jumping stride.

Two parallels at 35ft (10.65m) apart allow two non-jumping strides.

Upright jumps are best jumped off a short, bouncing stride, but consideration must be given to the distance between jumps in order that the jump 'in' helps to produce the length of stride required to meet the jump 'out' correctly. Parallel fences to the

34

horse appear as uprights, so here again one must have plenty of impulsion contained between the hand and leg so that the horse has enough energy to make the height and the spread.

A vertical jump to a parallel at 25ft (7.6m) apart allows one non-jumping stride.

A vertical jump to a parallel at 35ft 5in (10.8m) apart allows two non-jumping strides.

Care must be taken with this type of fence that the horse does not become too impetuous. The upright fence will appear relatively easy to him, and if he comes on too long a stride he may flatten over the first element and knock it, while concentrating too much on the second. If the fence is a cross-country one and is therefore solidly built, it will not fall down, and this could result in the horse having an unnecessary fall. It is imperative that the horse learns to jump these fences obediently and calmly, and always to look at and concentrate on the next obstacle to be negotiated.

A vertical jump to a spread at 24ft 6in (7.5m) apart allows one non-jumping stride.

A vertical jump to a spread at 35ft (10.65m) apart allows two non-jumping strides.

The same problem could occur here, though it is easier for the horse to jump a graduated spread fence than a true parallel. The important thing is to jump the first element well, landing on a balanced stride, so the horse meets the second element comfortably.

A parallel to an upright at 25ft 6in (7.85m) allows one non-jumping stride.

A parallel to an upright at 36ft (11m) allows two non-jumping strides.

A parallel to a spread (staircase type) 24ft 6in (7.5m) allows one non-jumping stride.

A parallel to a spread at 35ft (10.65m) allows two non-jumping strides.

A parallel to a spread at 24ft (7.3m) allows one non-jumping stride.

A parallel to a spread at 35ft (10.65m) allows two non-jumping strides.

All the above fences provide a parallel fence on the way in:

approach the first element as though it were an upright, with plenty of impulsion. Remember to keep your head up and look forward to the second fence, and then you should meet the second element comfortably. (Do not, of course, start teaching your horse to jump combination fences beginning with parallels until he is confident over low upright fences).

A spread (staircase type) to an upright at 26ft (8m) provides one non-jumping stride.

A spread (staircase type) to an upright at 37ft (11.3m) provides two non-jumping strides.

These distances should be regarded as suitable for an average 16-hand horse. Naturally the length of an individual horse's strides must be assessed to arrive at the best distances for these combination fences — here the length of stride is taken as 9ft (3m). It is of course better first to practise with distances which are tailored to your horse so he may learn to jump combinations which are comfortable for his particular stride before progressing to more exacting work by the lengthening or shortening of the distances. The horse must learn to be adaptable over combinations, and to trust your instructions, if he is to compete successfully. Before competing in a one-day event, you will walk round the course on foot. Pace out distances in combination fences, so you will know whether to jump off a short or long stride.

It is essential that you practise over grids at home. When simulating a show-jumping grid, begin with a small fence about 2ft 6in (76cm) in height. Continue with easily distanced and varied types of fence, increasing height and spread as confidence, of both horse and rider is gained. When your horse is able to jump show-jumps with confidence, the time has arrived to teach him to jump cross-country fences. I find telegraph poles ideal for teaching the horse to respect solid fences, though they are rather hard to come by. If possible, they should be adjustable, so that while they appear solid to the horse, they can in fact be raised or lowered, or moved to make a long or short distance. I am very fortunate in that near home we have a schooling facility with a grid of telegraph poles, placed at varied distances which can be positioned as low as 18in (46cm) or as high as 3ft 6in (1.1m).

Before beginning any work over solid fences do make sure that your horse is suitably dressed. It is likely that he will knock himself should he make a mistake, so he must be well bandaged or fitted with leather brushing boots. Over-reach boots should also be worn in case he becomes a little unbalanced when jumping and strikes himself. If you use exercise bandages, they must be stitched to hold them securely in position: tapes are not secure enough.

Training the horse to jump cross-country fences

If the horse has had a season's hunting and has been successful with the schooling exercises mentioned in the previous section, jumping cross-country fences should not cause him any problem at all. The most important factor to remember is to make everything easy for the horse at each stage. Introduce him to small fences only at first. If you can arrange for an experienced horse to be schooling with you at the same time, so much the better — if the young horse becomes worried or afraid, the older horse may be called upon to give him a lead.

For variety, you may have to visit several friends or acquaintances' establishments and beg to school over their cross-country fences. To begin with, the smaller the fences the better. Once the horse learns to jump a small ditch, coffin, drop fence or hedge without fear, he will be able to progress with confidence to the bigger and more formidable fences. Working in this way the horse should become so bold that he feels capable of tackling anything that you care to put him at. Do not gallop at any of these fences when schooling, try to keep the horse balanced in a controlled trot or canter so that he is able to see what he is being asked to jump and to learn to negotiate all obstacles without fear.

For all cross-country schooling it is important that the horse is well-protected. He needs leather brushing boots all round and over-reach boots, to prevent injury if he knocks a fence. A surcingle over the top of the saddle to keep the saddle secure and in place is also important. The rider *must* wear a crash helmet when schooling. I cannot overstress the importance of a crash helmet. So often one meets young riders schooling in an ordinary hard hat or no hat at all. The risk of head injuries is just as great at home as in competitions. In fact the risks when schooling are often greater than when actually competing, as a novice horse learning to jump cross-country fences is not going to jump them as safely or as well as an experienced competition horse.

Unlike show-jumping, where there are only four main types of fence, in cross-country you may come across innumerable variations of fence, requiring the horse to be very athletic, obedient and able to jump from a gallop or a short bouncy stride, and indeed sometimes from trot. Any cross-country course will produce most of the following obstacles, and before attempting cross-country competitions your horse should be schooled over the following:

Bullfinch This is a brush fence, solid at the bottom, with fine brush through which the horse must pass. Many youngsters try to jump over the top! Some horses dislike this type of fence at first because they cannot see over it to the landing side.

Post and rails These come in all sorts of variations, as straight rails, a combination fence, or as a parallel.

V- or corner fence This is a more difficult question for the rider, in my opinion, than for the horse. If the horse is between the rider's leg and hand it should not cause any problems.

Ditch: open type Many horses are worried by ditches, so make sure that the first one you put the novice horse to is small.

Ditch with rails in front or behind Often this type of fence does not cause as many problems as a ditch on its own.

Drop fence The horse must be strongly between the rider's leg and hand and should be allowed to look down, while the rider remembers to keep his own head up.

Steps These do not usually cause any problems.

Hedge or bush fence Your horse will have probably met this in hunting.

Water This needs to be handled with care, and I find the best way is to have the novice horse following an older horse the first time.

Another cross-country obstacle, the table fence. This should not be difficult for a horse that has been taught to jump spread fences properly.

A corner fence. This is the type of obstacle that should not be tackled until both horse and rider are jumping confidently over smaller fences.

In competitions, fences have wings or clear edges; on this training course the rider aims to clear the upright centre post of this post-and-rail fence.

4 Your first competitions

Hunter trials and cross-country competitions

Once the horse has had some initial jump schooling and has been introduced to cross-country obstacles in his schooling programme, hunter trials may be commenced. I find them an excellent way of furthering the novice horse's cross-country experience. The jumps are mostly natural obstacles, and the course will be similar to the cross-country phase of a one-day event. Again, if you are going to compete in hunter trials for the first time, ask someone knowledgeable to help you make the entry for the competition and to advise you on the appropriate dress to wear and the equipment necessary for your horse. Many hunter trials are organized by local hunts, so hunting dress is required: other competitions are organized as straightforward cross-country fixtures, in which case you may wear a stock, sweater and crash helmet. With regard to saddlery, you should read the schedule carefully, although all normal jumping equipment is usually allowed: *boots, martingales,* and *snaffle, pelham,* or *double bridle* – whichever your horse goes best in. (Although stronger bits are allowed I hope that your horse is able to go in a snaffle, with perhaps a running martingale fitted if he tends to become excited and carry his head too high.) Make quite sure that your horse's girths are secure and that all your equipment fits well. A *surcingle* round your saddle is an extra safety precaution when jumping.

If you are entering for a cross-country competition, walk the course on foot at least twice, better still three times. Keep the red flags on your right and the white flags on your left. Other markers, such as yellow arrows, are direction markers only. You will have to pass between two markers to start and then again to finish; failure to do this will cause your elimination even if you have ridden a faultless round.

The first time you walk the course look for general points and walk the track you will actually ride. On the second walk round, look at each fence and decide how you intend to ride it — the approach, take-off and landing. On the third walk round look carefully at any fence or track which may not be straightforward.

In such competitions as these it is a mistake for the young horse to go too fast. It is better to incur time faults than to risk refusal or a 'run out', or even a fall, because your horse is going at an uncontrolled gallop. The canter pace is most important over such courses, and a smooth, unhurried ride will add to both horse and rider's confidence.

Hunter trials are normally held in the spring or autumn, and should be treated as an excellent schooling ground for the event horse, rather than as a competition which you want to win, as at this stage the horse will not be ready to be hurried.

A little show-jumping

There are numerous show-jumping competitions held throughout the country all the year round. For our purposes, a local competition with a course of fences no more than 3ft (1m) high in the first round will be most suitable.

Walk the course carefully before the competition begins, pacing out the distance between combination fences, taking into account the types of fences used. A difficult combination to be tackled is that which comprises two uprights. For example, a gate to single rails may be used, with a distance of 24ft (7.25m) between. If this combination is jumped well, it will allow for one non-jumping stride between the two obstacles. The problem is presented by the horse which approaches the first element on a long stride and makes a big and wide jump over it, so that he lands too far into the space between the jumps to allow a comfortable stride before reaching the second element. Thus he gets too close to the second jump and then jumps awkwardly in his attempt to get out without knocking it down. The rider should bring the horse to such a jump in a short, bouncing stride and make the take-off close to the first element, which will help the horse to jump the second element easily. Many faults are incurred as a result of badly ridden corners. If the horse does lose thrust and impulsion in this way he becomes 'flat' in his canter, hollows his back and trails his hind legs, so that he fails to gain the necessary impulsion and jumps flat.

Having walked the course and realized your problems, the next procedure is for you to declare your intention to jump by entering and to have your number put down on the board. I think at this stage it is better to position yourself so that you are able to see several riders compete before attempting your own round.

Next prepare your horse and yourself. You will need a hard *hat, shirt* (or *choker* in America), *tie, breeches, boots, jacket* and a short jumping *whip*. Your horse will need *studs* (small ones all round), *over-reach boots, brushing boots*, and his usual *tack*. As soon as possible, mount your horse and go to the practice area. Jump him two or three times, first working him in at trot and canter, making sharp transitions so that he is really awake and listening to you. Then await your turn to compete. When you enter the ring, give the horse a sharp canter round the ring, listen for the bell and then begin your round. Even if you have jumped a clear round, do not jump off against the clock at this stage. It is far more important that your young event horse learns to jump clear rounds, so make much of him for his effort and take him home.

An inviting fence jumped as part of the show-jumping phase of novice horse trials at Crookham. The horse wears protective brushing boots.

The dressage competition

By now your horse should be going well in his basic paces and moving forward calmly and obediently. It is important to remember that all the time the jump training has been taking place the flat schooling must continue. Indeed, to my mind much of the jumping is only dressage until you leave the ground, as in all phases we are asking for obedience, impulsion, steadiness and balance. I suggest now that you enter for a small dressage competition – perhaps a Riding Club or Pony Club one. Follow your routine as closely as possible on the day before the competition, so as not to disconcert the horse in any way with unusual activities. Clean and check the tack for safety, inspecting all the stitching and ensuring that buckles and girths are sound. The bridle you use in the competition must be a snaffle, perhaps with a drop noseband; no martingales or boots will be allowed.

On arrival at the dressage meeting check to ensure that the horse has travelled well and safely. Locate the secretary's tent to declare your intention to compete and collect your number. Find out which arena you are to ride in and whether the competition is running to schedule or whether it is behind time. With this information you will know how long you will have to ride your horse in to settle him down after his journey. Always allow yourself plenty of time, so that at no point leading up to the competition are you rushed or flustered by any last-minute hitch, as this feeling will communicate itself to your horse.

The working-in period is very important. Ride in a relaxed manner, working the horse so that he becomes attentive and obedient. The time you allow for this depends on the temperament of your horse. If he appears to settle down in the atmosphere of the show ground, allow about twenty minutes' work. If he is an excitable type, he may require as much as an hour and a half of work before he is really settled. Try to keep calm yourself, even if the horse fusses, so that when you actually enter the arena you will be able to produce the best performance from your mount that he is capable of giving at this stage of his training.

After your test, slacken the girth and make a fuss of your horse

Part of the novice dressage phase. Make sure that the horse is introduced to the white markers at home so that they do not make his attention wander.

by feeding him some grass. Return him to his box, remove his tack and put on his headcollar. Give him a drink, and a short feed.

As your horse is eventually to become an event horse, and will therefore have a lot more work to do after the dressage test, it is important that he becomes accustomed to arriving for his dressage test in a calm state, and with the minimum amount of working in. If he is by nature rather excitable, you will have to be extremely patient and keep taking him to dressage meetings, competing until he becomes so used to them that he is unflustered and can give of his best with only a short period of working in. It really is worth taking trouble with the dressage phase, for a good dressage test will help you in horse trials as much as the cross-country and show-jumping phases. All three phases need to be practised individually, giving you and your horse the opportunity of improving your performance where it is weakest until you are equally confident during all phases. Taking the horse to small competitions limited to just one aspect of his training, so you can both concentrate fully on the one job in hand, will give you experience that should prove invaluable later in your eventing career.

Preparing for Pony Club and Riding Club events

Pony Club and Riding Club events usually take place in the summer months, from June through to August, with the Riding

Club and Pony Club championships being held in late August or early September. Ideally, you should have been able to purchase your horse some six to nine months earlier than the eventing season, during which time you will have continued his basic training, taken him hunting and also included some unaffiliated local dressage and jumping competitions. In fact all the work so far discussed in this book should be covered before you embark on your first one-day event.

Fitness is also very important for your horse, both mentally and physically. For these first events the horse does not need to be as hard and fit as he will need to be for the B.H.S. or U.S.C.T.A. trials later on, but it is important that you establish a regular routine. This routine will include feeding, mucking out, bedding down and complete grooming, which is normally known as 'strapping'. Work the novice horse for about one to one and a half hours a day, excluding his (and your!) rest day, to keep him healthy and fit and to prepare him for the competition that you wish him to enter.

The fitness programme for a Riding Club event will take approximately two months if you have to begin on a completely unfit horse. The best form of exercise in the very early stages of a fitness programme is walking. This helps to develop all the muscles without overstraining the horse. Later, work at the trot will help to build up the big muscles of the horse's body and limbs, while slow canter work will strengthen the horse's stomach muscles and improve respiration. The ideal way to work your horse is to ride him for up to an hour and a half at the walk and steady trot, with an occasional canter. In this way the horse will be using all his muscles to their best advantage without becoming overtired.

If you have already been riding and schooling your horse as I have suggested, then he will be semi-fit, but you may be beginning with a recently acquired horse which has been kept at grass and not ridden and is therefore in 'soft' condition. The horse is said to be in soft condition when he tends to fat and has no well-developed muscles. In this condition he will be unable to work for long without sweating and blowing a lot. The horse must be introduced to work gradually. His feed should not include many

46

oats, but mainly hay, properly damped. Remember to dampen the hay by tipping a bucket of water over the haynet, then hanging the haynet outside the stable for about half an hour for the water to drain off. In his first week the horse will need only about half an hour of walking a day, which may then gradually be increased. By the third week a little trotting may be introduced. As his hay is reduced to about 17lb (7.8k) concentrated food – nuts and oats – should be increased to between 8 and 10lb (3.5 to 4.5kg). In this process of bringing him into good condition you should make a special point of inspecting the horse each day for any irregularity in his condition, perhaps a cut or injury, and any apparent loss of fitness. I cannot stress too much the importance of gradual training. If you try to work your horse too hard too soon after his long rest period he will quickly lose condition and perhaps suffer injury or strain. To bring him into hard condition the horse needs sufficient work combined with a carefully balanced diet. In this way fat is turned to muscle, muscles and tendons are toned and the capacity of heart and lungs increased.

For a Riding Club event I like the horse to be able to canter without a break for a full six minutes at a speed of approximately 15 miles per hour, and during the latter part of your fitness programme you should gradually build up to this. In the last week before an event he will also need a short 'pipe opener' to clear his wind. This is best done the day before the competition, beginning first in a slow canter for about 200 yards (183m) gradually easing the horse out for a further 200 yards (183m) to a maximum speed, over the next 300 yards (274m) quietly slowing down to a canter, and then resuming walk until the horse's respiration rate has returned to normal. The recovery rate of the horse's respiration after a short gallop is a good indicator of his state of fitness. The breathing of a fit and healthy horse should return to normal after approximately five minutes. This recovery rate will vary with different horses, but if it takes as long as ten minutes, which is much too long, the horse is not sufficiently fit for his event. The horse in healthy condition should have a temperature of approximately 100.4°F (38°C). His pulse rate will be 35 to 40 beats per minute; his rate of respiration about 12 to 15 per minute.

Throughout the novice horse's fitness programme it must be remembered that he is still learning. He should begin each day with a little dressage training, being worked firmly forward in the basic paces. To add variety to the work this may sometimes be done in an indoor school or outdoor sand manège and sometimes while out hacking, if you can find a suitable open space. On two or three days each week he should be schooled in a dressage arena, so that he is used to the boards, practised at making a straight entry and halt. Ride the various movements, but do not ride the actual test; you will be surprised how quickly the horse can learn the test, and anticipate the various changes of movement. On two or three days a week you should also continue with your gymnastic jump training, working over poles on the ground, doing simple exercises to increase the horse's athletic ability and suppleness. Once a week, if possible, continue introducing new experiences in the way of cross-country fences. Try to arrange to take your horse to competitions during the three weeks before the first event, including a hunter trial, a dressage competition and if possible a show-jumping competition. These individual competitions will show you where there are any weaknesses in your horse's present stage of training, and will give you time to work a little more intensely on these aspects of his performance.

In a Riding Club or Pony Club event the dressage phase always comes first, but either the show-jumping or the cross-country phase may follow. It is usually easier for the novice horse to perform his dressage and show-jumping first and go cross-country last. I have found that very often with the young horse if he is asked to go cross-country before the show-jumping phase, he often gets a little on to his forehand, becomes unbalanced, and may then be careless in his show-jumping round. The cross-country phase is also the most gruelling, and a tired novice may well find it difficult to give of his best if the show-jumping phase comes last.

Preparing the event horse for a journey

To compete in events you may have to travel considerable

48

distances at times, very often staying away overnight. It is important, therefore, that your horse is completely at ease with the procedure of travelling and is relaxed when in transit. Here are some pointers that should help you.

Your horse will need protective *bandages* or *boots*, a *tail bandage* and *tail guard, knee caps, over-reach boots*, a *cotton rug* in summer or a *wool day-rug* for winter journeys, with a *roller* and a piece of *sponge* to go underneath the roller to prevent it pressing on his spine; a *headcollar* and a *rope*. When actually loading it is better to put a bridle on the horse as you have a little more control than with a headcollar, and it is easier for you to direct the horse firmly. I usually dress the horse in all his travelling equipment, with a headcollar, and then simply put the bridle on top so that I can slip it off when I have the horse in the box or trailer.

Position the box or trailer by a gate or hedge where a wing will be formed on one side. Place the ramp on an incline so that the angle for entry into the vehicle will be slight. Make sure the

Travelling boots being fitted to the event horse about to go on a journey; these protect the legs from a knock or other injury while in transit.

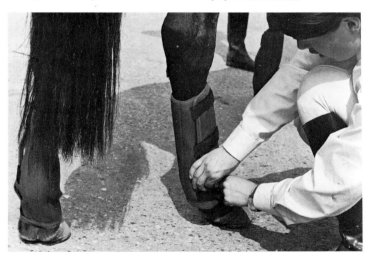

interior is not dark by positioning the box in such a way as to get maximum light outside, and letting down the ramp at the front — but keep up the chest bar. Load such things as feed, haynet and overnight equipment before you load the horse. When you are ready, walk the horse to the box and straight up the ramp. Do not hesitate, but do not rush him. Remain close to his shoulder without either looking back or getting in front of him. If you are able to walk the horse inside, have your assistant attach the rear strap promptly if you have a trailer, to prevent the horse reversing out again the moment you have him inside. If you have a horse box, ask your assistant to close the partition door quietly behind you. Then tie the horse up, making much of him as you do so, and remove his bridle.

If it is an overnight journey to your event, the horse may have a haynet to travel with. If your event is on the same day, then it is better not to travel the horse with a net, but to take one with you for the return journey. The horse will not be able to gallop across country on a full stomach, and hay is particularly bulky. In all this seek the help of a person experienced in loading and travelling horses until you have had considerable practice yourself.

When travelling the driver should be more than usually careful to drive smoothly, in order to give the horse as comfortable a ride as possible. Changing gear more frequently than usual will make the going smoother, and driving slowly, especially on corners, curves and at roundabouts will avoid the need for sudden braking. Try not to give the horse a valid reason for being nervous of entering the box in future! A horse which is worried about loading* and the subsequent journey will become tense and excited. In such an unsettled state he will not do well in competitions, particularly if a dressage test is required.

Care of the horse after a competition

It must be stressed that even at Riding Club and Pony Club level,

---

*A confident, well-trained and trusting horse should not give difficulty loading unless he has previously had a nasty experience. Some horses are nervous of travelling, however; more detailed hints on how to cope with this situation are given in *Training Explained.*

After the cross-country phase the horse should be allowed to graze and
dry off, protected against catching a chill by the sweat rug.

eventing is a strenuous sport. Throughout each phase keep a
careful eye on the horse for signs of stress, cuts or injuries.
Assuming all has gone well, it is after the cross-country phase that
the competitor must be particularly aware of the condition of his
horse. So often one sees a tired but exhilarated rider galloping
through the finish on a long rein and out of control, pulling the
horse up suddenly and risking a strain to the tendons, and then
failing to get off the horse's back until after a chat with friends. I
do hope that none of my readers are this type of competitor – or if
you are that you will quickly mend your ways! After the cross-
country phase pull the horse up quietly, dismount, slacken your
girth, throw a sweat rug over the horse's back and walk him until
his respiration is normal. If it is a very hot day, as it may well be in
the summer months, walk the horse for two minutes with his
saddle on and then remove it to sponge down the horse with
warm water, taking excess water out with a sweat scraper, and
then walk him until he is quite dry. Remember to check for any
cuts or injuries. He may then be returned to the horse box to be

rugged, offered a drink and given a haynet. Prepare your horse for the return journey as carefully as you did when you left home, putting on boots, bandages, etc. as before.

The day after

Pay particular attention to your horse's feeding, as the excitement of the previous day may cause him to go off his feed. First thing in the morning trot the horse in hand and check for any sign of lameness; he may well be a little stiff in his joints today. Examine the horse again for any cuts, and feel his legs for any sign of heat or swelling, and if you find any seek advice from an expert. If he is lame or there is excess heat or swelling, call in the veterinary surgeon. Do not work your horse the day after he has been to any event or horse trial; just lead him out in hand for about twenty minutes to help wear off any stiffness he may be feeling. The next day he may take light exercise, perhaps a little dressage schooling or a hack, and on the third day he will be ready to continue his normal training programme.

5 Training for your first major event

For your Riding Club and Pony Club events and local competitions the horse should be sufficiently fit to cope with the work asked of him. Assuming that your one-day events and local competitions have been a success, the horse should now be ready to start a systematic training programme for his first official B.H.S. or U.S.C.T.A. event.

A training programme arranged over a period of twelve weeks, and also a feed chart, may be found on pages 56 to 61. The question of the size, type and temperament of the horse is of course very important and no fixed rules can be made. I have based my programme and feeds on an average horse, three-quarter bred, standing at 15.3 to 16 hands. Naturally, if your horse is larger or smaller than this, then adapt your feed chart accordingly; you may also need to adjust it if your horse is excitable, or a poor doer, or is in any way below or above average. It must, however, be remembered that no horse under 15 hands is eligible to compete in official events in Britain.

The best way to use the chart is to display it where it is near to hand and can be marked off daily – perhaps in your feed room or tack room – though I usually put mine in the kitchen, where it can be checked regularly.

Horses appreciate a regular routine of exercise and feeding, but the timetable itself must of course fit whatever is most convenient for you. Try, however, to set a routine and adhere to it, bearing in mind that your horse will do better on three or four feeds a day. His first feed must be early in the morning, say at 7.30am and his last feed at 6.30pm. You will notice from the feed chart that I have made the first feed fairly small so that he is able to digest it well before you begin your exercise and schooling at around 9.30am. A horse will perform well and benefit from his schooling if his diet is suited to the work required of him. The first four weeks of the training programme should make the horse 'big' in condition, with the work at the canter in later weeks turning his flesh to muscle and making him fit to run. There are three very important rules to observe whatever form the diet of the horse is taking:

1 Feed little and often.
2 Water the horse before feeding.
3 Never work a horse when he has a full stomach.

Horses have small stomachs compared with those of other animals of a similar size, and a large quantity of water consumed after feeding can cause colic. As well as his regular daily feeds the horse should be given good quality hay between feeds. This also helps to relieve boredom, as it necessitates visits by you to the horse.

It should go without saying that you will feed your horse the best quality food. Plenty of succulents in the diet are also helpful – I have found it very beneficial with my event horse to feed fresh apples, carrots, swedes, and in the first six weeks to turn them out for a little grass for about an hour each day. As well as giving them a chance to let off steam, this helps to relieve boredom, assists with maintaining condition, and tends to have a calming effect on the impulsive horse. It must be understood, however, that if your pasture is not good and the fencing weak, then it would be better not to turn the horse out at all, and you can compensate for his lack of grass by cutting him a little fresh each day and adding it to his daily feed allowance.

From the training programme you will notice that I lay great emphasis on his dressage training. This is because the novice horse is still learning and improving and this basic training is in my opinion essential for his future success. If the horse is able to perform a good and accurate dressage test, commanding favourable marks, it will mean that to be successful the pressure on the show-jumping and cross-country phases will be less great. His daily schooling programme must also consist of plenty of slow work up and down hills to improve his balance and the use of his shoulders. A certain amount of road work is advisable to harden the tendons. His jump training will also continue in this programme and you will see from the chart on page 59 that on certain days I have recommended jump schooling as well as dressage training.

The evening before the horse's rest day give him a bran mash with 4oz (113g) of salt added, and also a handful of oats and 1lb (230g) carrots. On his actual rest day I usually feed two short feeds only, one at 7.30am and one at 6.30pm, and at the remaining feed times give 3lb (1.4kg) hay.

In this way his system has a rest from hard food. On two days a week make him a boiled feed. I usually feed this in the 6.30pm feed. The boiled feed should be made up of whole oats, barley and linseed. A good way is to soak the oats, barley and linseed the evening before in cold water, which will soften the seeds. At approximately 3.30pm the following day place the oats, barley, and linseed into a large metal container, fill with water to cover the seeds, bring to the boil, and simmer for two hours. The food is then ready for the horse — but let it cool until it is only just warm before offering it to him.

Introduce as much variety within your training programme as is possible. One way of doing this is to vary the place that you do your dressage schooling. For instance you may be able to work sometimes in an indoor school, sometimes in a sand manège, if the going is good in an open field or, nearer the time of the competition, in a dressage arena laid out on grass. Jump schooling can be varied in much the same way, particularly if you have friends who will allow you the use of their facilities. Cross-country schooling is a little more difficult and much will depend upon what you have available. I find it better to school over special types of fences rather than jumping them as a course — working on drop fences one day, for example, another day on coffins, and if possible giving plenty of attention to work over ditches and water.

Training and feeding programmes for a novice event horse competing in his first B.H.S. or U.S.C.T.A. trial

The training programme given overleaf is worked over a twelve-week period. At the beginning of the twelve weeks the horse is in light work, and is therefore able to cope with dressage schooling immediately. Turn to page 61 for instructions on feeding over the same twelve-week period.

JUNE
Week 1
Monday
20 minutes dressage, $^1/_2$hr road exercise (walking)
Tuesday
20 minutes dressage, $^1/_2$hr road exercise (walking)
Wednesday
20 minutes dressage, $^1/_2$hr road exercise (walking)
Thursday
20 minutes dressage, $^1/_2$hr road exercise (walking)
Friday
20 minutes dressage, $^1/_2$hr road exercise (walking)
Saturday
20 minutes dressage, $^1/_2$hr road exercise (walking)
Sunday
This is a rest day, so the horse is walked in hand for 20 minutes only.

Week 2
Monday
$^1/_2$hr dressage, $^1/$hr road exercise
Tuesday
$^1/_2$hr dressage, $^1/_2$hr walking and 5 min trot, on roads
Wednesday
$^1/_2$hr dressage, $^1/_2$hr walking and 5 min trot
Thursday
$^1/_2$hr dressage, $^1/_2$hr walking and 5 min trot
Friday
$^1/_2$hr dressage, $^1/_2$hr walking and 5 min trot
Saturday
$^1/_2$hr dressage, $^1/_2$hr walking and 5 min trot
Sunday
Walk in hand for 20 minutes.

Week 3
Monday
$^1/_2$hr dressage, $^1/_2$hr road exercise (walking), 10 minutes at trot
Tuesday
$^1/_2$hr dressage, $^1/_2$hr road exercise (walking), 10 minutes at trot
Wednesday
$^1/_2$hr dressage, $^1/_2$hr road exercise (walking), 10 minutes at trot
Thursday
$^1/_2$hr dressage, $^1/_2$hr road exercise (walking), 10 minutes at trot
Friday
$^1/_2$hr dressage, $^1/_2$hr road exercise (walking), 10 minutes at trot
Saturday
$^1/_2$hr dressage, $^1/_2$hr road exercise (walking), 10 minutes at trot
Sunday
Walk in hand for 20 minutes. Apply leg wash to strengthen tendons.

Week 4
Monday
$^1/_2$hr dressage, $^3/_4$hr road work
Tuesday
$^1/_2$hr dressage, $^3/_4$hr hill work
Wednesday
$^1/_2$hr dressage, $^3/_4$hr hack on tracks and road
Thursday
$^1/_2$hr dressage, $^3/_4$hr hill work
Friday
$^1/_2$hr dressage, $^3/_4$hr road exercise
Saturday
$^1/_2$hr dressage, $^3/_4$hr hack on tracks and road
Sunday
Walk in hand for 20 minutes. Apply leg wash to strengthen tendons.
Use saline solution on back and girth area
(may be necessary daily).

For a small drop fence the young horse should be allowed to look down,
but the rider must remember to shift weight onto the knees and keep the head up.

As part of the show-jumping phase of a one-day event, a young rider jumps a parallel fence with good style.

JULY
Week 5
Monday
$^1/_2$hr dressage, $^3/_4$hr road exercise
Tuesday
$^1/_2$hr dressage, $^3/_4$hr jump schooling
Wednesday
$^1/_2$hr dressage, 1hr hack, hill and
road work
Thursday
$^1/_2$hr dressage, $^3/_4$hr jump schooling
Friday
$^1/_2$hr dressage, 1hr road exercise
Saturday
$^1/_2$hr dressage, 1hr hack, hill and
road work
Sunday
Walk in hand for 20 minutes.
Continue as before with leg wash
and saline solution.

Week 6
Monday
$^1/_2$hr dressage schooling, 1hr hack,
road and tracks
Tuesday
$^1/_2$hr dressage schooling, $^3/_4$hr jump
schooling
Wednesday
$^1/_2$hr dressage schooling, $^3/_4$hr cross-
country practice
Thursday
$^1/_2$hr dressage schooling, 1hr hack
Friday
$^1/_2$hr dressage schooling, $^3/_4$hr hill
work for balance
Saturday
$^1/_2$hr dressage schooling, 1hr road
exercise
Sunday
Walk in hand for 20 minutes.

Week 7
Monday

$^1/_2$hr dressage, 1hr road exercise
Tuesday
$^1/_2$hr dressage, $^1/_2$hr jump schooling,
$^1/_2$hr hack
Wednesday
$^1/_2$hr dressage, 1hr cross-country practice
Thursday
$^1/_2$hr dressage, 1hr hack on roads and
tracks
Friday
$^1/_2$hr dressage, 1hr hill work
Saturday
$^1/_2$hr dressage, 1hr road exercise
Sunday
Walk in hand for 20 minutes.

Week 8
Monday
$^1/_2$hr dressage, 1hr hack, roads and
tracks
Tuesday
$^1/_2$hr dressage, 1hr jump schooling
Wednesday
$^1/_2$hr dressage, 1hr hill work
Thursday
$^1/_2$hr dressage, jump schooling
Friday
$^1/_2$hr dressage, 1hr hack
Saturday
Take to dressage competition
(preliminary or novice)
Sunday
Walk in hand for 20 minutes.

AUGUST
Week 9
Monday
$^1/_2$hr dressage, $1^1/_4$hr hack
Tuesday
$^1/_2$hr dressage, work on open spaces,
include canter for sustained period,
and $^3/_4$-mile hand gallop.
Road exercise to finish
Wednesday
$^1/_2$hr dressage, $1^1/_4$hr roads and tracks

59

Thursday
$^1/_2$hr dressage, jump schooling
Friday
$^1/_2$hr dressage, canter work for
sustained period, over $^3/_4$-mile
hand gallop. 20 minutes walking
exercise to finish
Saturday
If possible, take to small hunter trial
Sunday
Walk in hand for 20 minutes.

Week 10
Monday
$^1/_2$hr dressage, $1^1/_4$hr road exercise
Tuesday
$^1/_2$hr dressage, canter work: sustained
canter for 5 minutes, then pipe opener
or gallop over $^3/_4$-mile.
20 minutes walking exercise to finish.
Wednesday
$^1/_4$hr dressage, jump schooling
Thursday
$^1/_2$hr dressage, 1hr hill work
Friday
$^1/_2$hr dressage, canter work as Tuesday
Saturday
If possible take to small show-jumping
or dressage competition
Sunday
Walk in hand for 20 minutes.

Week 11
Monday
$^1/_2$hr dressage, $1^1/_4$hr road exercise
Tuesday
$^1/_2$hr dressage, canter work: 6 minutes'

sustained canter; $^3/_4$hr hack
Wednesday
$^1/_2$hr dressage, $1^1/_4$hr roads and tracks
Thursday
$^1/_2$hr dressage, canter work and hacking
as Tuesday
Friday
$^1/_2$hr dressage, $1^1/_4$hr road exercise
Saturday
$^1/_2$hr dressage, $1^1/_4$hr roads and tracks
Sunday
Walk in hand for 20 minutes.

Week 12
Monday
$^1/_2$hr dressage, $1^1/_4$hr road exercise
Tuesday
$^1/_2$hr dressage, sustained canter work
and pipe opener. Hack to finish.
Wednesday
$^1/_2$hr dressage, 1hr jumping schooling
Thursday
$^1/_2$hr dressage, canter work and hacking
as Tuesday
Friday
Travel to event, dressage and working in
Saturday
The first novice horse trial
Sunday
Walk in hand for 20 minutes.

SEPTEMBER
Week 13
Monday
1hr only hack
Tuesday
Continue with programme as before

The horse should be asked to do three or four events, then rest over the next few months, and begin his serious training again in January to be ready for the spring events in March. In the spring season we hope he will gain some points, and when he has had sufficient experience upgrade to the intermediate level. It is, however, a mistake to try and win in your first few events. I feel that the novice horse needs the experience of at least six events completed before he upgrades.

Suggested feed chart for horse standing 15.3 to 16 hands:

Weeks 1 and 2

7.30am	2lb (1kg) rolled oats, $^1/_2$lb (250g) bran
11am	2lb (1kg) hay (given after exercise)
1pm	2lb (1kg) rolled oats, $^1/_2$lb (230g) horse and pony cubes; $^1/_2$lb (230g) bran
4pm	2lb (1kg) rolled oats, $^1/_2$lb (230g) bran, $^1/_2$lb (230g) horse and pony cubes; 1 measure of vitamin supplement
6.30pm	3lb (1.4kg) rolled oats, $^1/_2$lb (230g) bran, $^1/_2$lb (230g) horse and pony cubes; carrots
8.30pm	12lb (5.4kg) hay

Weeks 3 and 4

7.30am	2lb (1kg) rolled oats, $^1/_2$lb (230g) bran
11am	2lb (1kg) hay
1pm	2lb (1kg) rolled oats, $^1/_2$lb (230g) racehorse cubes, $^1/_2$lb (230g) bran
4pm	2lb (1kg) rolled oats, $^1/_2$lb (230g) bran, $^1/_2$lb (1kg) racehorse cubes, vitamins
6.30pm	12lb (5.4kg) hay

Weeks 5 to 8

7.30am	2lb (1kg) rolled oats, 1lb (450g) racehorse cubes
11am	2lb (1kg) hay
1pm	2lb (1kg) rolled oats, 1lb (450g) racehorse cubes
4pm	2lb (1kg) rolled oats, 1lb (450g) racehorse cubes
6pm	3lb (1.4kg) rolled oats, 1lb (450g) racehorse cubes
8.30pm	12lb (5.4kg) hay

Weeks 9 to 12

7.30am	2lb (1kg) rolled oats, 2lb (1kg) racehorse cubes
11am	2lb (1kg) hay
1pm	2lb (1kg) rolled oats, 2lb (1kg) racehorse cubes
4pm	3lb (1.4kg) rolled oats, 2lb (1kg) racehorse cubes
6pm	3lb·(1.4kg) rolled oats, 2lb (1kg) racehorse cubes
8.30pm	10lb (4.5kg) hay

Boiled feed may be fed on two evenings a week, and in the first six weeks of the training programme the horse may be turned out for an hour to grass instead of feeding 2lb (1kg) of hay.

Stable management for the event horse

Good stable management is of the utmost importance in the preparation of any event horse. It is not enough to adhere to the training and the feed chart alone. It is essential that the horse is well groomed, and has a clean, well-ventilated stable in which to live.

The stable should be 12ft × 12ft (4m × 4m) if it is to house a horse of 16 hands. It must be light, airy, well ventilated, but completely free from draughts. The stable door is best in two halves so that the horse may look out over the top one. The bottom door needs to be 4ft (1.2m) wide and 4ft 6in (1.4m) high, with a bolt on the top and the bottom of the lower half door. The top half of the door must also be fitted with a bolt, as well as with a clip to hold it back against the outer wall of the stable and prevent it from blowing in the wind. The floor must be dry and clean. Vitrified blue bricks make a good floor surface, but these are unfortunately rather expensive; a concrete floor can work as well provided you have the top a little rough to prevent the horse from slipping.

With regard to bedding, I prefer to have my event horse kept on wood shavings or peat, as I find they are less likely to eat it. Some horses find straw (especially oat straw) extremely palatable and since it becomes increasingly important to be able to regulate the amount of bulk food consumed as the training programme progresses, straw beds can cause problems.

Below is an outline of a daily routine which may of course be adapted to suit individual needs, but which does incorporate the work training schedule already discussed.

7am   Inspect the horse to see that he has sustained no injury during the night. Give him fresh water, put on his headcollar and tie him up. Clean out the stable and put down a fresh bed. Pick out the horse's feet, fold his rugs back and give him a quick brush over. Sponge his eyes, nose and dock with separate sponges. Feed him, giving him the smallest hard feed of the day.

9.30am   Remove rugs, saddle up and exercise the horse, as laid down in the work programme, possibly for 1 1 hrs.

11.0am   Unsaddle and water the horse. Tie him up and groom thoroughly, remembering to keep a rug over his back in cold weather except when you are grooming that area. Put day rugs on the horse, refill his water bucket, fill a haynet with a measured quantity of hay and give to the horse. Pick up any droppings, set fair his bed and leave the yard tidy. Attention to your saddlery may be given here. If there is time, clean it and check stitching for safety; this may have to be finished after lunch.

1pm   Give the horse his second feed. Skep out stable if necessary.

2.15pm   Remove all droppings, pick out the horse's feet, refill water bucket. Remove day rugs and put on night rugs, checking horse's limbs as you do this for possible strain, heat, or injury. Clean remaining tack.

4.0pm   Check water. Feed.

6.30pm   Check water. Give last short feed. Skep out.

8.30pm   Final inspection of stable, check rugs, water bucket and bedding before shutting up the stable for the night.

To keep the horse in peak condition he should be thoroughly groomed every day. Grooming is an essential part of his fitness and health programme, as it tones him up — it is not simply for the sake of appearances. Pick out his feet several times a day to ensure that they are kept free of stones, mud, manure, etc. Use the *dandy brush* for removing grease and mud from the coat, but not on the tail or mane. It is a stiff brush and so it must be used gently over the coat of a ticklish or fine-haired horse, and when the horse's summer coat is through. The *body brush* will remove scurf, dried sweat, grease and dust from the horse's coat, mane and tail. This brush is an essential tool for the event horse. The *curry comb* should be used to clean the body brush, after every few strokes. Use the *water brush* to dampen down the mane and tail, to make the tail hang better and the mane lie flat. You will need three *sponges*, one each for cleaning the eyes, nose and dock; and a mane and tail *comb*, for trimming, cleaning and removing any tangles. Do not be too forceful when using the comb, as apart from causing the horse discomfort, it is possible to tear the hair. A *stable rubber* will give the coat a final polish. The *wisp*, made of a rope of hay, is used to promote circulation and generally to tone up the horse by massaging his muscled areas. For an event horse undergoing a conditioning programme, up to twenty minutes' 'banging' with a wisp will make a considerable difference to the tone of the muscles. The whole grooming routine is important, and a good length of time should be allowed for it. Properly carried out, grooming will improve the human's circulation as well as the horse's — if it is not hard work, you are not doing the job properly.*

When preparing a horse for eventing, I usually take his pulse, temperature and rate of respiration at grooming time. In this way I know what each individual horse's normal temperature, pulse and respiration are, and find that any deviation from normal is a good guide to the horse's general state of well-being. It is very simple to make a chart of the horse's temperature, pulse and respiration when at rest, and also immediately after work, and in this way establish when the horse has returned to normal. If any signs of stress are shown, you have an instant yardstick, and the problem can be dealt with immediately.

It is up to you to know your horse well in his stable. Get to know his habits, feel his legs and the quality of his coat constantly so that any signs of ill health or filled legs are spotted straightaway. If the horse is off colour, his work schedule must stop. Let him rest, put him on his rest diet, and mark on your chart when you had to stop and the exact day work was resumed. In this way you will be able to keep a systematic training programme functioning.

If your horse is prone to filled legs it may be necessary for him to wear stable bandages when standing in. Bandages are normally used to protect the horse's legs, for strengthening and support, for keeping the horse warm and if necessary to keep a surgical dressing in place. In the stable woollen bandages are best. They are fitted below the knee and go right over the fetlock joint. Begin the rolling-on of a bandage just below the knee or the hock, continue unrolling clockwise downwards over the fetlock and pastern, returning upward to the starting point. Bandages can be secured by tying the tapes in the middle of the cannon bone preferably on the outside of the leg, but never on the tendons. Do not bandage too tightly if you are putting on stable bandages.

* A more detailed procedure for grooming is outlined in *Stable Management Explained.*

If your horse is prone to leg problems, which I hope for eventing he is not, it may be necessary for you to use exercise bandages. Exercise bandages are used for support round the cannon bone, but do not cover the fetlock joint. Once support bandages have been used the horse will become accustomed to them. He will expect to have them on, so they will be needed in all jumping exercises and events. They are not used for the sake of appearance, in spite of what some young people seem to think as they fit bandages badly on their horses! If they are not used for their proper purpose they can do more harm than good. The exercise bandage must be secured by sewing. Tapes are not secure enough, and may well come undone; sometimes a horse has been known to suffer a slight strain to his tendon because the bandage tape was too tight and put pressure on the tendon itself.

6 Preparing for the event

Shoeing

As a general rule your horse's feet should be seen by a farrier (blacksmith) at least once a month to check that they do not become too long, though some horses need to be shod every three weeks. You will soon learn how often your horse will need to have his feet trimmed, and when a new set of shoes will be required, and you will be able to plan ahead accordingly. I always arrange to have my horses shod some four days before a competition. It gives them time to become used to the new set, and should by any misfortune a horse be lame after shoeing, with a prick or nail bind, there will be enough time to call your farrier back to rectify the problem.

It will be necessary for your horse to wear studs. Studs can be fitted by the farrier or screwed in by yourself when you need them, as long as you have asked the farrier to put stud-holes in the outside heels of the shoes when he makes them. The permanently fitted studs are not really suitable for competition horses, and studs that you can remove as soon as they are not needed are also safer. Studs give the horse security on difficult ground as they are anti-slip and various types are manufactured for riding under different conditions. They are used to give the horse grip, and thus confidence for jumping, and to enable the horse to progress at all paces up to and including full gallop over all kinds of terrain. If the ground proves very heavy and muddy, all shoes should have screw-holes, and large, square studs be used. If on the other hand the ground has been made slippery through a heavy shower of rain, pointed studs on all four feet should be employed. If the ground is considered perfect, with some spring in it, use small studs for work outside on the flat and in the dressage phase of your event. For show-jumping I prefer the large dome-shaped studs on each shoe, while for the cross-country phase I use similar studs but in the hind shoes only.

Jumping a log pile on a practice cross-country course; the
author has directed her horse at the centre of the obstacle.

The hayrack fence. Notice the different angle of elevation from the
jump above: this horse has to clear a wider and higher spread.

The water jump. This should always be approached very slowly and with caution, but with the necessary impulsion for the jump-out.

Above and below: Both these obstacles, the chair and drain pipes, are solid and should be taken with care. This type of fence needs a bold approach; the novice event horse should not be presented with solid obstacles until he is able to jump smaller fences with ease.

Another solid obstacle, a staircase fence. Notice the red flag which should always be on your right at the fence.

When the studs are not in use, the holes should be kept free of any grit and dirt by packing them with wadded cotton wool soaked in a little hoof oil. On the day before the competition the holes should be cleared of the old wadding and replaced with fresh, so that on the day of the competition this can easily be removed when you want to screw in studs. The horse should not travel with his studs fitted, because there is a serious risk of injury if he slips and treads on himself.

As a precaution I always have a spare set of shoes for my horse. At the beginning of the event season ask your farrier to make a spare set of shoes for you, complete with screw-holes, and keep them in the box that travels with you to all competitions. Most events have a farrier in attendance, and while it can waste valuable time to have a new shoe made, if you have a spare set it is a simple matter for the farrier on the showground to replace a cast shoe for you. In your tack box you should also have a full set of small studs and a full set of large studs, as well as spares of both types, cotton wool, a spanner, tap, and a small shoeing nail to remove the cotton wool from the screw-hole.

Studs being fitted into the screw-holes on the hind feet for the cross-country phase; they should be removed after the event.

Trimming

Careful trimming will improve the appearance of all types of horse, and besides this may help you in the dressage phase of a one-day event. Although marks are not actually awarded for turn-out, appearances do count in that the overall impression is important if good marks are to be achieved.

The hairs of the mane and tail will pluck more easily when the pores of the skin are warm and open, that is after exercise or on a warm day. Some horses will fidget, and pain may be caused if pulling is done in very cold weather when the pores of the skin are closed. The mane is normally pulled to thin out an over-thick mane, to reduce a long mane to the required length, or to encourage the mane to lie flat. The longest hairs from underneath should be dealt with first and removed a few at a time by winding them round your fingers or a metal mane comb, and giving a quick, sharp tug. The whole operation need not necessarily be completed at one time; indeed, I feel it is better to allow two or three days to finish the process. Never pull the top hairs, nor any that may stand up after plaiting because they will form an upright fringe on the crest. On no account must scissors or clippers be used for this purpose. A tail is pulled to improve its shape and appearance, and to show off the hindquarters. Tail pulling is also done by plucking out the hairs, beginning at the top of the tail and underneath, and working all the way down until a good shape is achieved. Again, pull only a few hairs at a time. The results of poor trimming can be fairly disastrous so it is as well to watch an expert at work before tackling your own horse.

Plaiting

The object of plaiting a mane is to show off the horse's neck and head. If your horse's head is naturally good-looking, small tight plaits will further enhance it. If your horse's neck is a little straight and lacking in crest or tends to be 'ewenecked' you can improve its appearance by clever plaiting. The mane can be plaited to give the illusion of more breadth if you brush it over to the nearside and

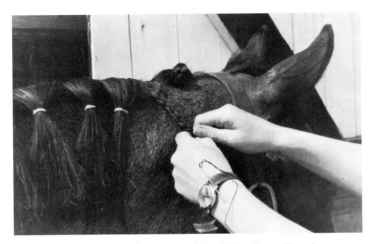

Plaiting the horse's mane before a competition. Notice the needle and thread which will secure the plait in place.

spray the top hair halfway down with lacquer, then brush over to the offside, plait and roll into neat knobs. The number of plaits will depend on the length of your horse's neck. A short-necked horse will look better with a lot of plaits whereas a long-necked horse needs fewer. Further details on the actual plaiting process are outlined in *Stable Management Explained*.

Further preparations before the event

Your tack should always be kept in good repair, but before an event check the stitching for any weaknesses with special care. It is not enough to have your usual saddle, bridle, numnah (if you use one) and girth; it is essential that you have spare stirrup leathers, three numnahs and two girths. I usually take two complete bridles, so that should I incur a fall and break some of my equipment I have a complete change quickly to hand. It is essential to have several changes of numnahs; these will certainly become wet and uncomfortable when the horse sweats, or in rainy weather.

So that there is no risk of you forgetting some vital piece of equipment, I usually draw up a list at the beginning of the season and keep it permanently in my horse box so I can check that I have everything I could possibly need. Here is the outline list that I use; you may want to add to it, but it will be helpful as a guide:

Fodder (remember if you have an overnight stay, that you will need enough for two days); two *haynets; water bucket* and *feed container;* mucking-out tools: *skep, fork, broom, shovel, muck sack; leather brushing boots* — four will be needed, and again a spare pair is a good idea; *bandages*, for travelling and also elastic ones for exercise; *gamgee* tissue; *rugs*, night rug, day rug, and a change in case they get wet; *sweat scraper, bucket* and *two large sponges;* complete *grooming kit; plaiting thread, needles, scissors* and *mane comb; stud tin,* plus *two complete sets of studs; hoof oil and brush; water containers* (it is essential always to take your own water: never water out of a common trough because of the possibility of disease communication.); *first-aid kit,* both for horse and for rider; *clothes and towels; disinfectant.*

When travelling to events it is essential that part of your equipment is a first-aid box for yourself, and also a box for the horse's requirements. You will not, I hope, be called upon to give first aid to your horse, but you should have the necessary items ready at hand in the box for a qualified person to do so. The horse's *first-aid box* should contain:

Thermometer; several *Animalintex* poultices; *wound powder; antiseptic cream; scissors;* crêpe *bandages;* roll of surgical *cotton wool;* surgical *spirits;* colic *drench; ice packs* in case of possible strain to a tendon (I use the sort sold in most large chemists for picnic hampers); *salt* — and any other items which your veterinary surgeon may suggest.

There are many pre-made kits for human first aid available at large chemists which contain antiseptics, plasters and bandage dressing, and I suggest you buy one of these to keep in the box. Remember that if you do have to use any item from either kit to replace it as soon as possible; it should always be useful and complete.

Your own equipment

This will depend on whether you are camping and sleeping in

74

your horse-box or caravan, or if the event is near enough for you to travel to on the same day. I will outline only the equipment you will need for each phase of the competition.

Dressage phase

Leather boots, socks, cream breeches, shirt, white stock, stock pin, black or navy coat, and a hard hat; a schooling whip for working in, which you may not use in the competition; a pair of spurs, which may be worn in the competition; gloves, dark-coloured, not white or bright yellow.

The stock would be a traditional type that is tied, which is something that you will have to practise at home to do well. Ready-made stocks do not look as neat in my opinion, and the point of the stock is lost. The prime reason for wearing the stock is not just because it looks smart but for supporting the neck in a fall. So often, too, one sees riders with new yellow or white gloves for their dressage, which is a shame, particularly with inexperienced riders, as it is an open invitation to the judge to notice your hands, and if they are not yet as quiet and steady as they should be you do not want to draw attention to them!

Show-jumping phase

You will need the same clothing as for the dressage phase, except that this time you may carry a whip, provided it does not exceed 27in (69cm) in length. In America the maximum length for the whip is 30in (76cm).

Cross-country phase

Here you will need to be dressed rather differently. You will need a crash cap, with a coloured shirt, stock, and coloured sweater, breeches and boots, and gloves. You may carry a short whip and wear spurs. Again, workmanlike colours are preferable to gaudy ones. The above are the bare essentials. It is wise to have a complete change of clothes for each phase in case of bad weather, or a fall. Those with long hair will need to secure it firmly and wear a hairnet, which looks neater and ensures that it will not blow across your face and interrupt your concentration.

7 The event itself

When you arrive

On arrival at the event do not unload your horse immediately. Look him over to make certain that he has travelled well and suffered no ill-effects from his journey, offer him a drink, and then set about finding your own bearings — locate the secretary's office, the dressage and show-jumping arenas, the conveniences and decide where it is safest to ride in the horse. When you do ride him around you will need as much space as you can get for any manoeuvres you may have to make. When you locate the secretary's tent remember to declare your horse as a starter and to buy a programme, which will have a map of the cross-country course.

Walking the course

It is important that you study the plan of the course in your programme and walk the course intelligently. Notice whether there are any combination fences and how they are marked, that is, if a series of fences situated closely together is marked la, lb and lc. If so, the series will be judged as one fence, which means you will be allowed two refusals in total at any part, as three refusals will mean elimination. If, on the other hand, a group of fences is situated closely together but is marked 1, 2 and 3 each section is judged as a separate fence, so you could have two refusals at each section and not be eliminated. Keep a particular eye open for direction flags and course markers — there is nothing more disappointing than to ride a good round and only then discover that you have been eliminated for going round the wrong side of a flag. The procedure that I hope you adopted when walking your hunter-trial course also applies to this phase of the one-day event. The first time look for general points and walk the actual track that you intend to ride; on the second and third walk round study each

76

Walking the cross-country course. This type of obstacle should be approached slowly, but with plenty of impulsion.

individual fence carefully, walking any combination fences and striding the distances between them.

When riding the course in the actual event, try to save your horse's energy by retaining your forward jumping position, taking the weight of your body mainly on your knees. Do not go flat out uphill; let your horse go at a faster pace downhill and on the flat where it is easier for him, though you should still remember to keep him between your hand and leg. After walking the course, return to your horse and remove all the travelling equipment from him. Fit the brushing boots and over-reach boots. His saddle and bridle should also be fitted while he is in the box. You should be wearing a hard hat and gloves. Now that you are ready for the unloading, get your assistant to unfasten the front ramp for the unloading so that your horse may be led out − even so, be alert yourself for anything in the immediate vicinity which may startle him in this unfamiliar place. As soon as he is unloaded mount him in a suitable clear space and go away and work him for about three-quarters of an hour. After his exercise, the horse may be put away in his horse box with a small net of hay, while you go to the secretary's tent to find out your starting times for the next day.

These times are usually posted outside the secretary's office after 4pm on the day before the actual event. As soon as you know your times you can begin to plan for the actual day of the competition, but first I suggest you drive your horse to where he is to be stabled and settle him for the evening. On arrival at the stables you will need to set fair his bed, remove his travelling equipment, groom him thoroughly, clean out his stud-holes and plug them with freshly oiled cotton wool, rug him for the night and give him a short evening feed. Try to follow your usual routine as closely as possible so as not to disturb him.

Stable chores

Having settled your horse you can now leave him to rest and begin to make preparations for the next day. Clean out your horse box or trailer so that it is ready to travel with your horse first thing in the morning. Clean your saddle and bridle thoroughly, and remember to take a last look at the stitching. Then using the list that I have already outlined for equipment required, pack the essential things so that they are readily available at the show-ground. Remember to fill your water containers afresh if you have had cause to use them already. Next check your personal equipment and clothing, clean your boots, and make sure that you have a clothes brush for your coat and hat for the event.

Having completed all your tasks, you should then return to your horse and make sure that he has settled in well and is not distressed in any way. He may need a further feed, and his evening hay at 8.30 as is your usual programme. If he appears a little unsettled and not wishing to eat his feed up, then make him only a very small feed, and do not leave it with him. Stay with him for a while so that if he does not eat it, you can give him a little hay instead. Take his temperature, and return to him in an hour's time; you will almost certainly find that he is just a little unsettled after his long journey. If you have any doubts, then call the veterinary surgeon as it is imperative that you do not compete with him unless he is one hundred per cent fit and healthy.

The day of the event

Whether you stabled your horse near the event for the night, or

78

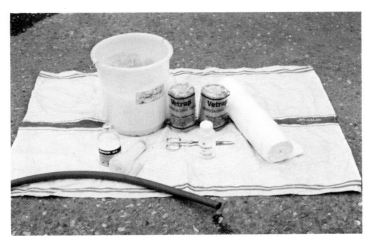

Above: Equipment for treating a severe brushing wound: a bucket of
Vaseline (to protect the heels against cracking); bandaging; gamgee;
antibiotic powder; penicillin; hose. *Below, left and right*: after cold hosing
to clean wound and reduce swelling, the gamgee is secured by a bandage.

Above and below: The water jump at a one-day event. These two pictures show one rider going into the water jump with confidence as he aims for the centre of the fence; the other rider is at the point of take-off; he has maintained impulsion to jump out cleanly at the other end.

are to travel from home on the morning it takes place, try to follow your usual routine as closely as possible. Go to the stables, check that the horse has not suffered any injury during the night, tie him up, muck him out, groom him thoroughly, and then plait his mane. Give him a short feed. By this time you will need your breakfast! On returning to the stables, dress your horse in his travelling equipment ready for his journey to the event, and load him carefully.

On arrival at the event, check to ensure that the horse has travelled well and safely. Collect your number cloth from the secretary's tent, find out which arena you are to ride in and whether the competition is running to schedule or is behind time. With this information you will know how long you will have to ride your horse in, to settle him down and loosen him up after his journey. Allow yourself plenty of time so that you, as well as the horse, are calm by the time your turn comes to compete.

Dressage phase
The riding-in period is very important. Ride in a relaxed manner, working the horse so that he becomes attentive. The time you allow for this depends on the temperament of your horse, and your previous experience with him will have taught you what

The dressage test requires calmness and concentration on the part of both horse and rider, and a riding-in period is essential.

suits him best. When you actually enter the arena, you will be able to produce the best possible performance from your mount that he is capable of at this stage of his training. If something goes wrong during the dressage test, try not to panic, but concentrate on getting the *next* movement right. After your test, dismount, slacken the girth and make a fuss of your horse by feeding him a handful of grass – no more, as he still has a very busy day ahead of him. Return to the box, and prepare to dress him for the show-jumping phase.

Show-jumping phase
Although your own clothing does not alter, your horse, however

Buckling the surcingle before the cross-country phase: this is an extra insurance against the saddle slipping.

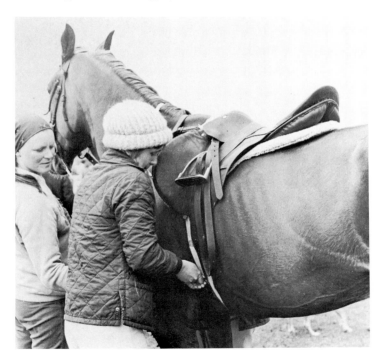

is permitted to change his tack after the dressage phase. Now is the time to fit brushing boots, over-reach boots, a martingale if worn, and of course a surcingle over the top of the saddle to keep it firmly in position.

The usual time allowed between each phase is half an hour, so this should give you just enough time to change your tack, have another last look at the course, and give your horse a warm-up. The most important preliminary to riding a course successfully is to walk the course thoroughly beforehand, so that you can envisage it as a whole and in the competition produce a flowing performance from fence to fence.

When jumping your novice horse over his first course of jumps at an event, you should remain unhurried and take from trot those jumps which you think he will jump better from a trot. Make wide turns so that the horse can maintain good balance. He may well be successful in his first competition and jump clear, which is all you need – so resist the temptation to jump him at speed. Speed will be important in the cross-country phase eventually, but not at your first competitions.

Cross-country phase
At the horse box prepare the following pieces of equipment for your return from the cross-country phase. I usually lay them out in an orderly line on the box that my tack travels in. *First-aid kit* for horse; two large *sponges*; *sweat scraper*; a bucket of warm *water*; *sweat rugs*, and a *jute rug*; *bandages* and *gamgee*; *stud tin* with tools to remove studs.

Check that your tack fits the horse well, and stitch the headpiece of the bridle to the horse's forelock, which will minimize the risk of losing your bridle if you have a fall. Change from your show-jumping clothes into your cross-country dress. If time allows, give the horse a short pipe-opener, which will help him to clear his wind and prevent him from having to waste time getting his second wind on the way round the course.

When riding the course, the canter pace is the most important for your novice horse. A smooth unhurried ride will add to your confidence in each other. Many competitors in their first

A good, well-controlled jump over a gate. The fitting of rubber or leather reins for wet-weather conditions stops them from slipping.

competitions make the mistake of going flat out round the cross-country course and, although your horse may be able to do this, inevitably at some point he will go too fast and have a nasty fall, incurring not only expensive penalties but also losing his confidence. In your first three or four events I believe it is more important that the horse has a good, steady round; only when he has had more experience should he be asked to jump at speed, so that he is able to jump clear without incurring time penalties. I would suggest that you wait until you are nearly ready to upgrade him before speeding up; ask it of the horse too early and you are likely to find you have wasted months of careful preparation. At the end of the cross-country course, dismount, slacken the girths, put an anti-sweat sheet over your horse and walk him in hand to cool and calm him. On your return to the horse box, look your horse over carefully for any cuts or abrasions he may have suffered during the ride. I usually sponge down the horse with warm water, using the sweat scraper to take out the excess water and sweat from his body, towelling dry his heels, ears, and face. Do not allow him to have a drink until he is quite cool, calm and completely dry. Remove the studs from his shoes. When he is completely dry prepare him to travel back to the stable where he will spend the night, unless you are intending to travel home that day, in which case prepare for your return journey.

Care of the horse after the event
On returning to the stable, give the horse a fresh bucket of water and feed a bran or linseed mash. (To make a bran mash, pour boiling water over half a small bucket full of bran and stir until all the bran is dampened. Cover with a cloth and leave until cool enough to eat). If the horse breaks out in a sweat at any time up to an hour later, it is most likely to be in those areas where he did not sweat in the first place. Dry the ears, throat and loins by using hay and then by rubbing a small area with the palm of the hand in the direction of the horse's coat. Begin where there is a dry area and

Washing down after the cross-country phase: this makes the horse cool and comfortable. Remember to check for cuts, bruises, etc. at the same time.

gradually move out of this area. If the weather is mild, you can also lead the horse out. Leave the horse to eat his hay while you clean his tack and the horse box. Then when you have finished take off the horse's rugs, replace them with night rugs, remove bandages, give him a feed, water and leave him. Later in the evening go to the stable to check that the horse is comfortable.

I cannot over-emphasise the importance of looking after your horse with special care when he has been competing. Remember that a one-day event is a very taxing ordeal for him, both mentally and physically, and he will be below par for forty-eight hours after the event. Handle him gently, check for injury, stress, or strain, feel his legs for heat and swelling, take his temperature and pulse. After forty-eight hours, if all is well, he should be able to continue his usual training programme. The day after the event should be a light and easy day for the horse. Check again that he has no injuries or swelling. Walk him in hand for twenty minutes only. It is likely that he will be stiff after yesterday's exertions, and a little walk to stretch his limbs will help him to unstiffen. If it is a fine and warm day, turn him out in the paddock for an hour, which will help him to relax. On any rest day, including this one, his short feed rations must be reduced to avoid any side effects.

Your usual schooling programme may be resumed on the third day. After the competition you will be able to take stock of your horse's present stage of training and begin to work harder on his weaknesses. In his training programme he should continue to work at his dressage, even if this has gone well. Eventually it is to be hoped that our novice horse will progress to intermediate competitions, where a slightly more difficult dressage test is asked of him. It is no use waiting until the horse upgrades only to discover that he has not sufficient training behind him to cope with the more advanced work. In any case, the more advanced the horse's training the greater success will he achieve as a novice.

8 Some veterinary problems

There follow some ailments from which your event horse can suffer. In certain instances I have mentioned my own treatment, but as a novice-trainer without experience, you should always seek the advice of a veterinary surgeon if your horse shows the symptoms I describe.

Sweating or breaking out

A horse may be found to break out in a heavy sweat some time after being brought into the stable after working and also after he has been thoroughly dried off. This excessive sweating is the result of nerves — it is a nervous reaction to work which the horse has found exciting. Try to bring the horse in from work as calmly as possible, going so far as to dismount and walk for the last half mile home if you have been working across country. After leading him in and unsaddling and watering him, give him his haynet, make sure that he is dry and warm, and later return to ascertain whether he is in fact settling down. The excessive sweating usually occurs on the neck, flank and behind the ears. It may help to use a nylon girth on such a horse to allow more air to get to the skin in this area where sweating is likely to occur. It will also help to loosen the girth when you dismount to walk in your horse.

Wounds

These may be any abrasion, cut or bruise inflicted by an external cause. In the case of the event horse it is inevitable that at some time in his training or competition career he will incur an injury. Basically there are four main types of wound: clean-cut, lacerated, bruised or punctured. Clean-cut wounds will bleed fairly freely, and are relatively easy to deal with. It is simply a case of stopping the bleeding, perhaps by cold hosing the wound. Apply a little antiseptic powder and keep the wound as clean as possible.

Lacerated wounds are a little more troublesome. They may be caused when jumping a cross-country fence, or perhaps by the horse getting caught up in wire when hunting. The problem with a lacerated wound is that it is more likely to go septic; again, cold hose, dress, and seek veterinary advice. A bruise is likely to result from a bang or blow, and is a somewhat more deep-seated injury that usually takes quite a time to develop and therefore to heal. I usually find that alternate hot and cold treatment is very helpful here — that is using an Animalintex poultice followed by cold hosing, followed again by the poultice, and continuing the treatment for at least forty-eight hours, and probably for three or four days. (See colour pictures on page 79 for cold-hosing treatment.) Strengthen the area finally by cold hosing for twenty minutes daily. Punctured wounds are pricks in the leg made by thorns, or sometimes from a nail picked up in the foot. The difficulty with a punctured wound is that it is very easily overlooked, as the skin is pierced by a nail, thorn, or other sharp object and then immediately becomes closed over. The best action is to poultice the area to draw out any septic matter. In all cases of wounds the horse must be immunized against tetanus.

Sprains and strains

As part of good horse management it is important that you observe your horse's legs daily in his stable before and after exercise. At any sign of heat, pain, swelling, or lameness, stop work immediately, poultice the leg and seek your veterinary surgeon's advice.

Colic

This is a severe stomach ache. The horse may sweat profusely, appear restless, look round at his stomach, and may try to lie down and roll. Call the vet immediately, who will give him a relaxing drug to ease the pain. If you suspect that your horse has colic, stay with him, keep him warm until the vet arrives, if he does try to roll, walk him in hand to keep him on his feet.

Brushing wound

This is an injury to the inside of the fetlock joint, where the legs knock against each other, thus causing an area of soreness. If you have followed my advice and used brushing boots, this should not happen; prevention is the best cure in this case. If by any chance your horse does incur a brushing wound, bathe it in salt water and dress with an antiseptic powder.

Bruised sole

This is normally caused by the horse treading on a stone or sharp flint. If possible, try to avoid this type of going. Should you be unlucky, stop work and apply a poultice to the sole.

Corn

This is a bruise at the angle on each side of the foot between the wall and the frog. It is often caused by leaving the shoes on for too long. The treatment is to have your farrier pare out the sore place, and then to poultice for two or three days. It may be necessary for the horse to be shod with a three-quarter shoe which is a surgical shoe which the farrier will certainly recommend if he thinks it necessary.

Worms

There are four main types of worms that a horse may have, which are absorbed into his system in various ways. If they are present in his system because of poor grazing, it is best to seek some advice from the vet on how to improve your pasture. *Red worm* is unfortunately common in young horses, and is a result of their grazing in a field which is, colloquially, 'horse sick' — infected pasture. The horse appears to eat well enough but still loses flesh, has a dry dull coat, is dull-eyed and subject to diarrhoea. Horses with red worm are sometimes also anaemic. Call in the veterinary surgeon for advice about diet and treatment. Sometimes worms can be detected in the horse's droppings. By a special process, the vet examines the dung and makes a fairly accurate assessment of the degree of infestation of these and other worms. *Bot worm* is known in equestrian circles as 'stomach bot'; the bot-fly is the villain. The horse appears to have a good appetite but does not benefit by it since he will suffer weight-loss, and have a dull and 'staring' coat. Stomach bot is a parasite produced by the bot-fly in pastures where a horse may graze. As the horse is grazing, the fly lays its eggs on his legs, and in licking them the horse absorbs them into his intestines where the maggot finally hatches out. The eggs, which are very small and yellow, may appear on the horse's legs during the spring and summer months. They can be clipped away and on the vet's advice a powder can be administered to the horse. Treat on professional advice only. The symptoms of *round worm* are few, but a horse suffering from this parasite may have attacks of colic, which you will be able to detect. These symptoms are usually accompanied by irregular bowel movement. Call in your veterinary surgeon for advice on diet treatment. The causes are again poor pasture and failure to remove droppings on a weekly basis. *Whip worm* is another type of worm that appears at the horse's rectum. The general symptoms are a yellow discharge under the root of the tail, and the horse will rub his tail on the wall or manger. Veterinary advice should be sought. Poor, stale grazing usually produces the conditions in which a horse contracts this, and here again if you have doubts about your own pasture and how to care for it, you should ask an expert to inspect your pasture and obtain his advice.

It is important in your fitness programme to watch your horse very carefully, particularly if he was kept at grass until you started his training for eventing. No matter how well you feed him or follow the training schedule, if he has a worm problem he will not be able to achieve good condition. As a matter of course I always worm all stable-kept horses every three months, using a different brand of powder or paste each time, which prevents the horse – or rather the worms! – from becoming used to one proprietary brand. If you are able to turn the horse out to grass for an hour or two each day, then I suggest you should step up your worming routine and worm the horse every month to six weeks.

Some further veterinary problems

When you first purchase your horse you should have him vaccinated against *tetanus* and *equine influenza*. With all ailments or diseases, prevention of an illness is better than having to find the cure. When a cure is necessary, valuable training time will be lost and the horse will take a long time before being brought back to peak condition. A competition horse will be more susceptible to these ailments than a horse which stays at home all the time and does not come in contact with other animals.

Tetanus is usually fatal. The disease is caused by the *bacilli tetani* which enter the blood stream through an open wound, sometimes through very small cuts or abrasions. In the excitement of competing it is possible to overlook small cuts or grazes and that is why I have stressed throughout this book the importance of inspecting your horse not only at home after his exercises, but also after he has travelled and especially after he has show-jumped or been round a cross-country course. Tetanus is more common in some districts than others, and areas of land which have a high clay content are known to have a higher incidence of the disease. When a horse contracts tetanus it has a temperature rise to 103°F–105°F (39.5°C–40.5°C). The membrane of the eye extends over the eyeball and the horse displays nervousness, standing with tail stretched out and head and neck held forwards and down. As the disease takes hold there will be overall stiffening of the legs, and the jaw will become firmly set, hence the colloquial name of 'lockjaw'. Of course, you must call in the veterinary surgeon at the earliest sign of any disorder, and if a horse is unfortunate enough to have contracted the disease he will have to be kept in a darkened box and put on a laxative diet. The vet would advise no hay and ready access to plenty of fresh air.

Equine influenza needs mention because no matter how well you care for your horse it may contract the disease. Some people will always disregard the risk of passing on the disease by attending competitions or other gatherings when their horse comes from a stable already infected with equine influenza. It is a highly contagious virus infection which can manifest itself in a coughing epidemic among several horses. The horse has a sudden rise in its body temperature, which may reach 102°F–106°F (39°C–41°C) in the early stages. This high temperature does not, however, last long, and for this reason the symptom may be overlooked and the contagion spread quickly through an entire stable. After the temperature rise the horse will begin coughing, with a dry and shallow cough which later becomes softer and more fluid. Call in the veterinary surgeon as soon as you can. The treatment is usually a course of antibiotic injections which your veterinary surgeon will administer, and naturally the sooner the course is started, the quicker your horse will be on the road to recovery and back to his training schedule. The cough may last for anything up to fourteen days. The horse will of course be taken off work, and put on a special non-heating diet. Training and exercise can be resumed only very gradually after the coughing has ceased altogether. It is worth arranging for the horse to have an anti-flu injection each year before the start of the competition season.

I hope my readers will realize now why I recommend the daily taking of the horse's temperature as part of one's fitness procedure. Not only does it show his normal state of health, but it will enable you to detect at the earliest opportunity any signs of possible infection or of the horse being off colour.

Sick nursing

Good nursing is very important, so at the first sign of ill-health call your veterinary surgeon. Next, ensure that your horse is stabled in a well-ventilated loose box, free from all draughts, and as far as possible, isolated from other horses. He will need a clean, deep bed of short straw or shavings. The loose box should have a half-door but the horse should never be in a direct draught, although fresh air is essential. Naturally the horse will have to be kept warm with proper clothing in the way of rugs and bandages. His box should be cleaned frequently and made fresh at all times. If possible, any medical treatment he receives should be carried out at the same time each day. Part of your nursing will be to keep the horse company, and if the horse is very ill he should not be left alone at all. If the illness is very serious you will have to ask a friend to help you in your watch over him in case of any crisis. Water should be changed frequently, to prevent it becoming tainted by the ammonia fumes of the stable. Do not remove all the horse's rugs, but quarter him — that is, fold back the front part of the rug to brush the horse lightly, then fold the back part of the rug forwards to brush his quarters. Hand rubbing is comforting to the sick horse and helps to relax him. After any period of illness, remember that the horse must be returned to work gradually, so consult your veterinary surgeon about this before beginning work with him again.

9 Around the next corner: the three-day event

If you are an eventing enthusiast, much pleasure can be gained from watching the more advanced horse trials. In Britain these take place from March until May, and then from August until October, whereas the season in America varies according to the regional climate. In particular, the three-day event is extremely popular as a spectator sport, and of course any of my readers who have been successful in their novice horse trials may have the ambition to compete in a three-day event. You will need to begin with a novice two-day or three-day event, and I suggest that first you watch two or three of these events, if possible acting as groom for an experienced event rider. A great deal can be learned by actually being in the field and helping out in this way.

The standard of fitness and training of the three-day event horse and rider has to be considerably more extensive than that of the novice horse. On the first day of a three-day event the dressage test is performed. This is a good deal more exacting than that of the one-day event and lasts about ten minutes. The horse must be able to perform lateral work – half-pass and shoulder-in – and be schooled to work in the collected paces. It will be appreciated that the horse has to be as fit as any racehorse to perform the speed and endurance phases, and it is no easy task to train him to be sufficiently obedient on the flat, when he is fit and ready to run! On the second day the competition is divided into four phases, all of which are timed independently. Phases A and C are endurance tests, the distances totalling between 6–10 miles (10–16km) over roads and tracks, with the rider using trot and hand canter as the main paces to achieve an average speed of 260 yards (240m) per minute. Phase B is taken over a steeplechase course comprising about four fences, which are jumped three times and may not exceed 4ft 6 in (1.3m) in height. The rider completes this phase at the gallop, speed playing an important part in the test. On the completion of Phase C there is a compulsory ten minutes' halt, during which the horse is examined by a veterinary surgeon and

The start of Phase D – the cross-country – at the Badminton Horse Trials,
the most taxing part of this famous three-day event.

other experienced people before being allowed to continue with
the next phase. Phase D, the cross-country, is the most taxing part.
The horse is expected to gallop 3 miles (6.5km) across country,
with fixed and solid fences. These fences are considerably more
formidable than the ones met in novice horse trials and require a
bold and experienced horse and rider.

In the United States Phases A and C are run over a total of 5–6
miles (8,000–10,000m) in the Preliminary Division, with the same
average speed as in Britain. In Phase B the solid part of the
steeplechase fences may not exceed 3ft (91cm), while a brush-type
fence may have a maximum total height of 4ft 7in (1.4m). In Phase
D the distance is from 2½–3 miles (4,000–4,800m).

On the third day, the final day of the competition, the ability of
the horse to jump a course of coloured fences is shown after two
very strenuous days. The fences for the show-jumping phase are
not very big, in fact no more than 3ft 6in (1.2m), but the course is
designed to test the horse's training and suppleness after a test of
extreme fitness on the previous day.

Many of you may never have the desire or the opportunity to
ride in a three-day event. It is, however, the ultimate stage of
training in the eventing world, and requires tremendous courage,
obedience and training on the part of both the horse and the rider,
who achieve a true partnership by the combination of their
individual skills.

95

Glossary of American Equivalents

Animalintex a poultice. Alternatives are antiphlogisten or numotizine

Chemist pharmacist or drugstore

Headcollar halter

Loose box box-stall

Over-reach boots bell-boots

Plaiting braiding

Racehorse cubes pellets

Roundabout traffic circle

Rug a sheet or blanket

Running reins draw reins

Spanner wrench

Sweat-rug sweat sheet or cooler (an over-size woollen blanket loosely designed for the cooling and drying-out process)

Acknowledgments

We are particularly indebted to Coakham Cross Country Club, Edenbridge, Kent for kindly allowing us to make use of their facilities for the photographs; to Miss Marie Stokes F.B.H.S. for her assistance and technical advice; to Candida Geddes for the benefit of her knowledge and careful observation in the preparation of this book; and to Peter Landon whose photographs have so enriched this publication.